ENGLAND TODAY
IN PICTURES

THE HOUSES OF PARLIAMENT
FROM WESTMINSTER BRIDGE

ENGLAND
TODAY
IN
PICTURES

WITH AN INTRODUCTION BY A. G. STREET

Contents

✶

Odhams Press Limited · Long Acre · London

A DEVON VILLAGE

Around the outskirts of Dartmoor are to be found some of the prettiest of the villages
of the West Country. Chittlehampton is typical with its church and old cottages.

4

Introduction

By A. G. STREET

THIS England of ours has been called many things in her time, some complimentary, and others the reverse. Here it is proposed to look upon her today for what she is—a legacy, the legacy that history has bequeathed to us. From new-born babe to he or she who has passed the scriptural landmark of threescore years and ten, each who is English bred and born is entitled to a goodly share in that valuable legacy.

Often it seems that we do not appreciate its value. Indeed, many of us sometimes seem to delight in belittling it. We extol the virtues of this country and that, but decry our own. We forget the good work that was done by our forebears, and the many difficulties and dangers that they overcame, preferring rather to accentuate the mistakes they made. That, of course, is the English way, the hopelessly illogical character of English people.

One part of today's legacy of history is a passionate national belief in the sanctity of the individual. The laws that he must obey are laws that he as a voter has approved. The police who enforce them are his servants not his dreaded masters. Should any wealthy or powerful man oppress the lowliest in the land unduly or unfairly, the oppressed can and does invoke the common law of England in his defence, and rarely does it fail him in his need.

How have the people of such a small country achieved and maintained their proud place in the world? By hard work? Yes and no. The truth is that English people are inherently lazy; they don't like work one little bit, but they can do it when the need arises. They are nothing like so industrious as many of their European neighbours, but somehow they get better results from their labours. How long they will be able to continue to succeed in this apparently lazy fashion is open to conjecture, but for nearly nine hundred years it has served them well.

During the first seven hundred years or so of that period their work was mainly concerned with two things—the land and the sea. Even today the ancient industry of farming ranks fourth in importance in England, both in the number of people whom it employs and the money value of its yearly production. But today instead of subsistence farming, food production for sale to townspeople is its main purpose.

Even in such a small country the differences of climate play their part in deciding the type of agriculture carried on in different districts. Broadly speaking the climatic line between wet and dry weather runs from the Humber to Weymouth Bay. East of that line the farming is mainly devoted to plough-land crops like grain that need fine weather for harvesting. West of it in the rainy districts grassland provides the home for the best livestock in the world.

Of course, war needs altered that division tremendously, compelling a beleaguered industrial nation in danger of famine to demand that its farmers should plough up their cherished pastures, and grow grain and potatoes in the wetter western districts. The farmers grumbled as was their English right, but they obeyed ; and, by the help of modern machinery and the willing aid of townsfolk of all classes and both sexes, fought and won half the Battle of the Atlantic by increasing home food production far beyond their own or anyone's expectations.

Once they had got the plough going they discovered that they were glad of the change. For there was too much grass. Between the two world wars an industrial nation had decided that it could dispense with home farming, and use its countryside merely as a playground during its leisure. In conse-quence, a green sickness had overtaken the countryside ; but in a couple of years of war, instead of the rural scene being one of green picked out with a few patches of ploughland, it became one of ploughland interspersed with a few splashes of green grass.

In the main, English farming of recent years has been devoted to producing the greatest weight of human food per acre ; but in addition new war-inspired crops have been planted. Flax was one of these, for linen was needed by all the fighting services, notably the Air Force. So the fields that many years before had grown the flax that became the sails of Nelson's *Victory* showed blue at dawn once again in order that the needs of our aerial fleet could be supplied.

What does the farming pattern look like today ? There is a definite increase in grassland, but this time it is mainly of a temporary character, being destined to feel the iron of the ploughshare every few years. Each district is being farmed as experience and present needs direct. In the vales and the water-meadows by the chalk streams cattle hold dominion. These are mainly native breeds, but wherever English sailors found a good class of cow overseas, English farmers imported them and improved them. So in every county can be found the black and white Friesians of Holland, the Channel Island Jerseys and Guernseys, and the lemon-spotted cockhorned Ayrshires and both Galloway and Aberdeen-Angus black-polled beasts that originally came from over the Border.

Of the native breeds red, white, and roan Shorthorns predominate in every county. Red Polls hold sway in East Anglia ; Red Devons rule Drake's countryside ; Sussex has its own breed of beef cattle ; Lincoln Reds are

6

ST. IVES BAY

Storm clouds gathered at sunset make a fine background for this group of fishing boats at St. Ives, Cornwall. This is one of the many small but important fishing ports in the far west of England, though perhaps it is more widely known as an artists' colony.

7

spreading everywhere; and the Marches of Wales boast thousands of those glorious Hereford cattle, red in body with white faces and dewlaps.

Pigs and poultry have been rapidly increasing in the last year or two, but sheep come next to cattle in importance, the different breeds having been originally developed to suit certain districts. Some are horned like the Exmoor; Leicesters are hornless with white faces, and Hampshire Downs are hornless with black faces. Agile Herdwicks graze on the fells of Cumberland, and Cotswolds thrive in that bleak limestone district known to its natives as the " Wot's Cold."

The greatest change in the rural scene effected in recent times is the increase in agricultural machinery in every parish. Today England boasts the most highly mechanized agriculture per acre of any country, over ninety per cent of its machinery being the property of its farmers, the remainder being owned by Government departments. Horses for pleasure are once again coming into fashion, but horses for work are rapidly giving place to tractors. Nearly every farming job is done by modern machinery—ploughing, threshing,

PAGEANTRY IN THE CITY OF WESTMINSTER

The State opening of Parliament by the King is witnessed by great crowds of Londoners and visitors to the city every year. The King and Queen still drive from Buckingham Palace to Westminster in a special coach drawn by cream horses. Along the route are men from Guards regiments. The ceremony is performed in the House of Lords.

AN OLD COUNTRY CUSTOM

May Day is still celebrated with traditional liveliness in many parts of the English countryside. The May Queen is crowned and taken in her carriage to the village green, where local inhabitants take part in a display of folk-dancing. Maypoles are rarely seen now, but here one is the centre of ceremonies on the green at Ickwell, Beds.

cutting, combine-harvesting, milking, even flax-pulling and hop-picking.

However, here again the illogical character of the English shows itself, enabling the new to mix with the old in most charming fashion. Thus the latest combine-harvester imported from America is housed during winter in an old tithe barn, while overhead amidst the rafters that ancient tool, the flail, is tucked away. In that pointed corner of the field where the tractor and binder cannot find room to manœuvre, an old-age pensioner wields his scythe at harvest time. Again, in the wet fen fields of Lincolnshire the graceful swinging arms of age broadcast seed in truly biblical fashion, what time the tractor and the combine drill lie idle in the cart shed.

So much for the land—what of the sea? Being an island people, with the sea for most of their boundaries, the English could not help being sailors. The first attraction of the sea was that it could provide fish for food, so the English farmers proceeded to harvest it. East Anglia's fishing fleet has always been manned by East Anglian farmers. In Elizabeth's day the Devon ploughboy turned his team on the headland, and the sea breeze brought him a sniff of salt water. This was such heady stuff that a few days later he was sailing with Drake or Hawkins. It is just the same nowadays. The East

9

AN ENGLISH CATHEDRAL

The Church has played a part of much importance in the life and development of England through many centuries. The old cathedrals of the cities and the village churches are among the nation's proudest monuments. Here is a striking view of Wells Cathedral in Somerset, one of the most beautiful, famous for its west front.

Anglian farmer-fisherman became a minesweeper during the war. The Devon tractor-driver also caught a whiff of ozone from the Channel; and found it such a pleasant change from the exhaust of his vehicle that before long he found that his corduroys had changed to bell-bottomed trousers, and that he was sleeping in a hammock instead of in a bed under the thatch.

So throughout her history England's sons went to sea, voyaging all over the world to fashion the legacy that we inherit today. They brought their law and their ideas of freedom into far-off lands. They took away their country's manufactured goods and exchanged them for the produce of the world; so much so that for many years past every English grocer's shop has contained currants from Greece, sugar from the West Indies, coffee from Brazil, tea from China, rice from India, wines from France, raisins from Spain, tobacco from Virginia, and countless other things, in reality hiding a map of the whole world behind its counter.

Why were the sailors from such a small nation so successful wherever they voyaged? Largely because they did not set out with any idea of conquering the world. Being islanders they perforce went to sea. In their travels they landed on strange shores, where in most cases they found a state of things that offended their ideas of what was fitting for human beings. So they stayed and put it right, not so much because they wanted the job, but rather because they had stumbled on it, and felt that it was up to them to do the right thing. Thus, without deliberate design they founded a great empire overseas. But, in conformity with the illogical character of the English, they allowed each part to govern itself, being free to support the Motherland in time of war or not as its people should decide. The result of that apparently absurd arrangement was a stronger tie than any fashioned by dominion and power; for the recent war showed the world just how strong it was, as once again the illogical English way triumphed.

It was primarily due to the work of her sailors that England became such a great industrial nation, processing the raw materials that their voyaging brought from every corner of the earth. The increasing prosperity this brought fostered a rapid increase in the population; for, as the business of the nation prospered, it required an increasing number of workers of all kinds to keep pace with it. In fact today almost everybody in the country serves his neighbours in some way or another.

An intricate network of railways enmeshes the whole country, providing the safest rail traffic in the world. Here again is to be found that English mixture of old and new, that is both charming and efficient. Each week sees new types of locomotives and rolling stock on the lines, flashing quickly past the older ones. But the latter still roll along and do their job, for England built to last in Victoria's day. Each month sees electric power ousting steam

OLD AND NEW METHODS

The use of machinery on the land has greatly assisted agricultural development, but science works together with the older methods. The top picture shows combine

ON THE ENGLISH FARMS

harvesters near Winchester ; these machines gather and thresh grain and tie straw in one operation. Below left : threshing and straw stacking ; right, raking hay.

13

A LAKELAND IDYLL

Girl walkers rest on a grassy bank in Borrowdale, a famous Lake District beauty spot near Keswick. Here the river Derwent takes a rocky course below the mountains.

in this stretch of line or that. The fast boat trains run from the main line stations to the port towns. The advent of the railways made the canal system of inland transport less important, but even today goods are barged along its ancient waterways, especially from London to Manchester and other Midland manufacturing towns.

Road transport today is a serious rival to the railways, lorries making long-distance hauls throughout the land. Many of these travel by night, and so a chain of transport cafés has sprung up along the main roads. Most of England's road system was constructed for horse traffic, but the higher speed of motor vehicles now necessitates the construction of wide arterial roads.

The latest competitor in the transport business, both passenger and goods, is the aeroplane. In such a small country this will not find it easy to oust either road or rail transport ; but will be a serious rival to shipping for overseas transport to other countries.

Another service that employs many people is that of communication by post, telegraph, and telephone. Mail trains thunder through the night from every main-line station, and their contents arrive at their final destination in all sorts of ways—by motor van, by postman on a bicycle or afoot, and even by Donkey Mail, for this still runs in Clovelly. Telephone and telegraph afford quick communication between town and town, town and village, lonely farm and town, and even from homeland to overseas countries.

In order of size and importance in England's industries that of textiles and clothing comes first, iron and steel second, mines and quarries third, and farming fourth. The years of war sadly disorganized all of them, and it needed long and sustained effort to get them into their peace-time stride again. Another industry, building, is of vital importance to them because it has to supply the necessary homes for their workers. For war meant not only that very few new houses could be built, but also that enemy action destroyed thousands of the old ones.

What of the people who inhabit this legacy of England ? Their different occupations and surroundings set their mark on them. The Cockney is alert, quick in his movements, volatile, and always witty. The farm worker is slow-moving, stolid, and possessed of a sardonic humour. Sailors and road transport drivers show the same wrinkles round the eyes, due to staring ahead into the night for long periods. Railway workers are very like farm workers in speed of movement and habit of mind. The trains go fast enough ; their job is to see that accidents are few and far between. Speech, of course, varies from county to county. From the " Wot cheer, mate ? " of the Cockney to the " How bist ? " of Dorset ; from the soft U of Devon to the harsher dialect of Northumberland ; and from the sweet " Love " and " Honey " of Lancashire to the rasping " Bor " of East Anglia.

But with all these differences of habit and speech English people from north to south and east to west have one thing in common—they will not permit anyone to throw his weight about unduly, no matter what his wealth or how high his position. Thus when Hitler began his Fascist salute, the London taxi-drivers hailed each other with it in derision. Years before the war, when the news reels showed Mussolini strutting across the cinema screen, audiences in town and country greeted him with derisive laughter. They subject their own leaders to the same salutary discipline, the colonel, the sergeant-major and the mother-in-law are traditional figures of fun on their music-hall stage. They elect a town council, and thereafter refer to them in conversation as the " town scoundrels." Should any politician even after a proven success get a trifle too big for his boots, the English will immediately vote against him and even their political convictions. For their chief conviction, and one that they will never relinquish, is that the moment any person shows that he thinks he cannot be done without, he must be done without lest worse befall.

Mainly because of this hopelessly illogical character of her people it is often said by others that a special providence watches over England, or rather that her amazing luck throughout history has been undeserved because she has never set out to obtain it. But that is the English way. Another example of it can be seen in the relationship between her people and her monarchy. No other people has such a passionate hatred of any form of dictation, and yet the English have kept their Crowned Heads. True, when one of these went too far they cut off his head and tried a republic for a while; but, finding this too dull and too dictatorial, they soon reinstated the older system.

Today the relationship between King and people is a very friendly thing. To English folk home is the keystone of life, be it castle or cottage, mansion or bungalow. Therefore, to them Buckingham Palace or Windsor Castle is merely the King's home, the house where an Englishman lives with his wife and brings up his family. The two Princesses are his children, and every commoner in England appreciated that those two children stayed in England throughout the war, and that the Royal Family shared with the people the dangers of the blitz.

That is why the home of democracy and freedom keeps its monarchy. The people's Parliament governs, but the King is still the Head of the State, and none would have it otherwise. So once again England mixes the new with the old in charming and efficient fashion. In his Christmas broadcast the King naturally uses the phrase, " My people ; " while the poorest mother in the land looks upon the two Princesses as " bonny children," and is as interested in their welfare as in her own children's.

It is the same with the English Church. Her people keep it—they don't know really why, but they do. But they insist that everyone in the land shall

A SCENE IN WESTMORLAND

Westmorland is one of the counties of which a large area comprises the beautiful English Lake District. Here is a typical scene in a valley between the fells which attract thousands of climbers and walkers. Local sheep thrive on the fell pastures.

ON THE CORNISH COAST

The scenery around the English coasts offers great variety, but nowhere are there cliffs of such grandeur as in Cornwall. Here are cliffs outside Polperro Harbour.

18

A YORKSHIRE DALE

The largest of the English counties is well known for long and lovely dales formed by the many streams which come down from the Pennines. Here is a view in Wharfedale.

be free to worship his God in whatsoever fashion he pleases. Westminster Abbey is still the setting for State religious services; cathedral spires still point majestically to the sky in every county; and an ancient grey stone church tower overlooks every village. But side by side with these in every parish can be found the churches and chapels of every religious denomination. Moreover, should the clergyman of any denomination attempt to dictate, the English will not destroy his church; they will merely refuse to attend it. Again, if the Established Church should fail to serve the needs of the people, its congregations will dwindle until the necessary lesson has been learned by its bishops and priests. But even so, English people will hesitate many times before they think of scrapping their Established Church, no matter what its sins of either omission or commission; because it is part of the old legacy, something that has been bequeathed to them by their ancestors.

But although the effect of two great wars in the life of one generation has been perhaps to loosen the hold of organized religion upon English people, they have still retained their love of pageantry and ancient customs. No matter whether the Government be Socialist or Conservative, the State Opening of Parliament by the King is carried out according to tradition. The Lord Mayor's Show is still one of the landmarks of London's life. The village rector still proceeds with his surpliced choir to the farmyard to hold the annual Rogation Service in the open air, surrounded by his parishioners of all

LIFE IN THE COUNTRY

Piped water from the country's waterworks does not as yet reach every hamlet. In old-world surroundings a villager and his wife draw the day's water supply from the well in their back garden. This scene of rural peace comes from Upperton, Sussex.

sects, to whom he preaches using a harvest wagon for a pulpit. Helston in Cornwall still holds its Furry Dance. Wishford in Wilts still celebrates Oak Apple Day. And in every county the hunt still rides in scarlet and top hats.

To sum up, in every aspect of their national life English people insist upon an apparently illogical mixture of old and new ; and perhaps the best example of this is to be found in the setting in which they live—the English scene. Go where you will, that pattern is a very lovely one.

The Scilly Islands and Cornwall boast flowers galore, but no trees worthy of the name, because the sea winds hold sway over this district. Devon varies tremendously, from the wilds of Dartmoor to the sheltered combes around it. Somerset boasts such green grass and such red ploughland. Eastwards to the Garden of England, which is Kent with its fruit and its hops, lies the chalk country, several counties of rolling downland interspersed with streams and water-meadows. East Anglia and Lincolnshire are famed for their plough-land farming. The Shires are the best grazing and the best hunting country in the world. The Vale of Evesham is another garden, much like Kent, and a sight in plum blossom time. Herefordshire boasts more horses and fewer cars per hundred acres than any other county. Cheshire is a land of cows ; Lanca-shire one of poultry. In between the manufacturing towns of the Midland counties the charm of farming England greets you on every side.

From the Cheviots to Southampton Water, and from the Wash to the Marches of Wales, the rural scene is clothed with a patchwork quilt of many colours. Each patch is of different shape and size and colouring, and the hemstitching between them varies according to the district. Wire fence, stone wall, hedgerow, and open dyke, all border every colour imaginable— green of grass, yellow of kale, blue of flax, salmon of sainfoin, burnt sienna of ripe clover seed, gold of wheat, ash-blond of ripe oats, and countless others.

The homes of the farming folk vary in similar fashion. Stone and slate in Cornwall ; thatch and cob in downland ; clunch in Norfolk ; stone and mullioned windows in the Cotswolds ; black and white in Cheshire ; and again stone, hard stone, in the north.

That setting is part of the legacy of history that has been handed down to the English of today. Obviously it was never planned ; it just happened as natural conditions and the needs of the times dictated. The other part is their proud place in world affairs. Their present problem is to find a way to be worthy of such a glorious inheritance, and to try to improve it for their children's children. The late Professor Lethaby's words would seem to be their motto for to-day. " To forget the past would be as foolish as to ignore the future. Behind is custom, as in front is adventure."

This book is a slight attempt to show in pictures that the next adventure will be worth while.

HARVESTING IN BERKSHIRE

The
English at Work

ALTHOUGH the great majority of Englishmen live and work in the large towns and cities today, agriculture still remains one of the fundamental industries of the nation. Farmers there will always be in England even though it is a hard life involving long and irregular hours of work. But the radio, the motor-car and the wider distribution of electricity for power and lighting have robbed the countryside of much of its former loneliness. Most work in the town offers regular hours, a measure of security, ample leisure and higher financial return, and all the blessings of modern civilization are at hand. Yet many a townsman in recent years has sacrificed these things to farm his own few acres.

A quarter of the whole population live and work in Greater London, the commercial centre of an Empire, and many up-to-date factories have grown up around its outskirts in the last quarter of a century. But the major industries of England are still largely concentrated in the North and the Midlands, textiles and iron and steel in Yorkshire and Lancashire, mining in Derbyshire and County Durham, pottery-making in Staffordshire, and so on. Many new industries have added to the national prosperity since the First World War, especially in chemicals and electrical engineering.

23

PLOUGHING BY TRACTOR

Heavy tractors plough up a steep hillside below Wittenham Clumps a famous landmark in South Oxfordshire. The wide use of tractors has considerably increased production.

PLOUGHING WITH HORSES

In spite of all mechanical contrivances, the horse is still indispensable to the farmer. This Lancashire team depicts the partnership of man and beast in soil cultivation.

Farming in the Vale of St. John, near Keswick

TENDING THE FLOCKS

From the Cheviots to the Sussex Downs sheep-farming prospers, and the shepherd is a familiar character on English hillsides. Top picture shows a flock of Southdown sheep by Clayton Mill. Below, an old shepherd tends new-born lambs on a downland farm.

SHEEP-SHEARING TIME

A shepherd is clipping the wool from one of his ewes in the old-fashioned way while his faithful dog stands by. On many farms in England nowadays mechanical shearing is used ; this makes for speed, but skill is still required to avoid injury to the animal.

CATTLE-REARING FOR BEEF AND MILK

Excellent pasturage has made England famous for beef and milk of the highest quality. Most districts have native breeds of cattle. Some breeds are primarily milkers; these include Jerseys, Guernseys and the black-and-white Friesians. Among the beef producers are Red Herefords and Devons and the hornless Aberdeen-Angus. The hardy Shorthorn, good for beef and milk, is the most useful cow to the average English farmer. Pictures opposite show milking by hand and by modern apparatus in Suffolk.

HARVESTING ON A

Corn is being cut on the slopes of Shaldon Hill, near the coast in Devonshire. Such scenes are familiar around the English countryside towards the end of summer, when

FARM IN DEVON

the reward of the year's labour on the land is gathered. The faces of some typical farm workers reflect the strong influence of their life-long association with the soil.

BRINGING IN THE HAY

Few activities of the farmer's year in England are so picturesque as the summer haymaking. Given a spell of fine warm weather the grass is ready for cutting from about the middle of June. But with the variable English climate haymaking, like harvesting, often has to be done with great speed between spells of showers. The farmer and his men work from dawn almost to sundown so that the hay is cut, gathered and stored in ricks or barns for winter fodder. These pictures from Salisbury Plain (left), near Alton, Hampshire (bottom left) and the Dorset Downs (below) show again how the horse plays an active role in work on the land.

BEAUTY IN THE ORCHARDS

Springtime transforms the orchards into a riot of colour which brings promise of heavy crops of apples, cherries, plums and pears. These scenes come from the Vale of Evesham and Kent, two important centres of fruit-growing. The man with the tractor employs modern methods to keep the orchard soil in good condition. Near Sittingbourne, in the Kentish fruit country, the roofs of an oast-house are contrasted with blossom.

CIDER-MAKING IN SOMERSET

Cider is the "wine" of the West and its production is an important industry of Somerset and Devon. Here a load of cider apples is transferred into the storage loft at Ansford, near Castle Cary. The hand press is still used (top right), though power operated machinery has largely replaced it. But the farmer samples his brew in the old way.

Daffodil harvest at St. Buryan, Cornwall

FEEDING THE GEESE

In the enclosures around the farmhouse and barns the farmer usually keeps his smaller
stock such as pigs, poultry and rabbits.   A girl is seen here feeding geese in a typical

IN THE FARMYARD
farmyard in southern England ; right, a peaceful scene in Sussex showing "Huggets Furnace" where, in the fourteenth century, the first English iron cannon was cast.

43

HARVEST SCENE IN THE

Against the background of romantic Kenilworth Castle, an ancient fortress famous in history and literature, the work of harvesting is seen in progress. This delightful

44

HEART OF WARWICKSHIRE

camera study comes from the Shakespeare country, which contains some of the best soil for crops of this kind. The farms of the district are both large and well kept.

HOP-PICKING IN KENT

Hops, which form the basis of the Englishman's glass of beer, have been cultivated in Kent ever since the Middle Ages. To-day the hop gardens cover many square miles of the country, the largest of them lying around Paddock Wood, between Tunbridge Wells and Maidstone. Every September the annual hop-picking brings hundreds of poor families from the East End of London to the lovely Kentish countryside. Stripping the laden hop-bines from early morning to dusk is a wonderful holiday for these Cockneys.

VILLAGE BLACKSMITH

HEDGER

CRAFTSMEN AT WORK

Old-time crafts still play their part in the life of village and farm, where many jobs depend on the inherited skill of human hands.   While the number of active craftsmen

THATCHERS

BASKET MAKER

SCYTHEMAN

IN THE COUNTRYSIDE

has greatly declined in the last thirty years, efforts have recently been made by local community councils to encourage and train apprentices to keep useful crafts alive.

49

CRAFTSMEN IN KENT

In a woodland near Ashford an old craftsman is cutting stakes for making sheep hurdles.
Below, a busy morning in a wheelwright's yard at Staple, a village near Canterbury.

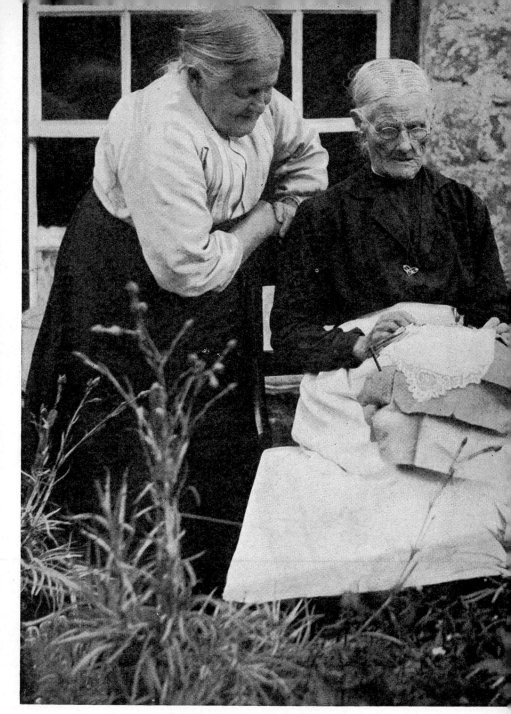

LACE-MAKING IN DEVON

Honiton lace is known all over the world. Many old ladies of this Devonshire town still practise the delicate craft in their homes. This lace-maker is eighty years old.

FELLING THE WOODLANDS

In Sussex and the New Forest men are felling timber and hauling it away to the mills.
Through the centuries England's forests have been cut down to meet timber demands,
but a nation-wide scheme of afforestation by the State is helping to repair losses.

STONE AND SLATE

England is unusually rich in natural deposits of building stone and there are hundreds of working quarries, large and small, scattered throughout the land. A great belt of oolite limestone running diagonally across England from Lincolnshire to Dorset has given this country some of its finest villages and churches. The famous Portland

FOR NEW BUILDINGS

Quarries (right) provided Sir Christopher Wren with stone for St. Paul's Cathedral and which has since been used for great public buildings throughout the British Commonwealth: the supply is still far from exhausted and the stone in great demand. On the left skilled craftsmen are seen splitting and trimming roofing slates in a village quarry.

CHINA-CLAY PITS

Cornwall has an important raw material, china-clay, which plays a great part in the manufacture of china and porcelain. Since it was discovered about 1750, the industry has developed rapidly and is very profitable nowadays. Some of the largest pits are, like the one shown here, situated around St. Austell in the south of the county where gigantic pyramids of the white china-clay add an unusual note to the landscapes.

TIN-MINING IN CORNWALL

The ancient tin mines of Cornwall, known to Phoenician traders over 2,000 years ago, once supplied most of the world with this metal. Discovery elsewhere of rich deposits which were more economical to work robbed the Cornish industry of much of its importance. But there has been a recent revival, and miners are again winning the metal from deep mines which sometimes run out for some distance under the sea.

COAL-MINING

Coal has been the main source of England's industrial prosperity during the past century, and coal-mining is still one of the largest and most important industries both for home and export needs. The miner's life is terribly hard and fraught with dangers, though many improvements in mining have been made recently. England's chief coal-fields are in the North Midlands, County Durham and Northumberland, while coal is produced on a smaller scale in Kent, Cumberland and the Forest of Dean. A striking view of a modern mine shaft in Derbyshire is shown on the left. After labouring at the coal face far below ground, the miners smile as they reach the surface after their shift.

Steel Works at Scunthorpe, Lincolnshire

IRON AND STEEL

Iron and steel, second largest of England's industries, employs a vast army of skilled workers, upon whom the masses depend for many of the everyday necessities of life. Processes in a steelworks are shown : top left, a white-hot steel section in a rolling mill ; below, casting the metal ; above, a steel-welder at work wearing a special helmet and gloves for protection against heat, sparks and the glare of the arc.

MOTOR MANUFACTURE

In the last thirty years the British motor industry has grown rapidly and mass-production of moderately priced cars has increased the standard of living of millions of citizens. English cars, unsurpassed for their quality and reliability, are in demand throughout the world and ably demonstrate our national aptitude in engineering skill. These photographs were taken of work in famous factories at Cowley and Birmingham.

AIRCRAFT CONSTRUCTION

England leads the world in the high standard of her aircraft production in which great technical advances were made through war needs. In these scenes from English factories are shown frameworks for fuselages and wings being assembled, above ; a flying-boat nearing completion, top right, and a radial engine on assembly line, bottom right.

This remarkable view taken from the air is typical of the scene in the great commercial pottery-making area of Staffordshire, often referred to as the Black Country of

THE POTTERIES

England.   On most days of the year, the outpourings of thousands of kiln chimneys cause a permanent blanket of smoke to hang darkly over these highly industrialized towns.

69

POTTERY MAKING

North Staffordshire is the centre of pottery manufacture and the name of Wedgwood, founder of the modern industry, is world famous. The craft of pottery design has long traditions in England, and apart from the town factories, many individual village craftsmen still follow the simple methods of their ancestors. Staffordshire turns out vast quantities of utilitarian domestic ware by machinery (picture right) ; but fine ornamental pieces are also produced by skilled artist potters on the time honoured wheel (below). Before new pieces are fired in the kilns a second time they are " dipped " in liquid glaze (left). At bottom right, girls are seen painting hand-made pottery.

COTTON INDUSTRY

The inventions of James Hargreaves and Richard Arkwright in the eighteenth century transformed a large part of the county into one of England's greatest industrial areas. Today the industry employs about half a million workers. Top left, typical factory

OF LANCASHIRE

chimneys in a Lancashire cotton town: right, a girl weaver at a loom. Below, left, building up a pattern of cloth on a machine prior to final loom process: centre, removing full tubes from spindles, a process known as d'offing: right, tracing a broken thread.

WOOLLEN MANUFACTURE

The manufacture of woollen yarn and cloth is a craft which dates back to medieval England. At one time the industry was widely distributed, and many West Country villages were famous for their cloths. Today it is concentrated largely in the West

IN YORKSHIRE

Riding of Yorkshire. Woollen mills after dusk make a striking picture at top left; right, dyeing yarn: below (left to right), cleaned wool being fed into a pneumatic conveyer; removing a top; a craftsman drawing a warp thread; setting up the warp for weaving.

CANNING INDUSTRY

Food canning, a large and growing industry, adds to the variety of the Englishman's diet. The wholesome preservation of fresh fruits and summer vegetables makes possible their enjoyment all the year round. Above, dehydrated fish is being packed; top right, a machine sealing tins of margarine and, bottom right, girls canning herrings.

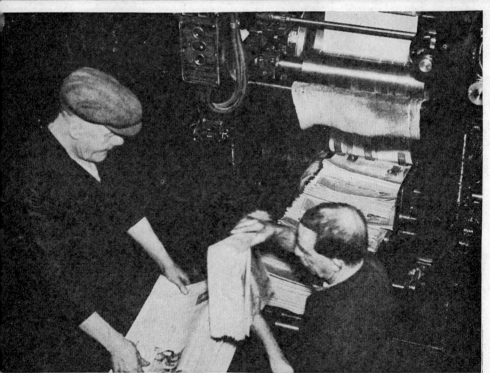

NEWSPAPER PRODUCTION

England may be proud of her long traditions in journalism, for several famous daily newspapers have been appearing regularly for a century or longer. The Englishman, rich or poor, likes to be well informed of world events, and besides the great national daily newspapers covering the whole country, every large provincial town has its local

AND PRINTING

*morning and evening journals. Here we see the editorial room of the " Daily Herald "
in London; an operator setting type by machinery (top right); the printed edition already
folded for the reader coming off the machine (below left), and great rolls of paper
being unloaded outside the works of a famous Sunday newspaper in London.*

LONDON STOCK EXCHANGE

The historic square mile that comprises the City of London is the hub of the nation's finance. Here in the shadow of the Bank of England is the Stock Exchange, the authorized market for dealing in or exchanging stock, shares and other securities. Stockbrokers also do business with their clients outside in the " Street "— Throgmorton Street, a narrow thoroughfare running down beside the Stock Exchange. (Picture above.) A busy scene in the " House " is shown on the left, the first picture ever to be taken within its doors.

NEW HOMES FOR THE PEOPLE

Between the two world wars millions of
new homes were built all over England.
the greatest housing developments taking
place around the large cities like London
and Manchester. New suburbs, garden
cities and model villages spread rapidly
and vast numbers of the English masses
achieved their dearest ambition—a home
and garden of their own. Great slum
clearance schemes were also pressed
ahead and in the industrial cities grim
and overcrowded Victorian tenements were
replaced by model workers' flats. The
Second World War interrupted housing progress and produced a shortage by far greater
than the first, but the Government have
plans well advanced for the greatest housing
drive in England's long history. Above,
bricklayers at work; right, early stages in
construction of a ferro-concrete building.

Sailing barges in the Thames Estuary

A Nation of Seafarers

RIGHT down the centuries the sea has played a great part in the life and development of England. It is natural that some of the world's greatest sailors and adventurers should have been Englishmen and that the nation's prosperity and greatness should have been founded upon maritime trade. The long traditions of the Royal Navy, which go back to the days of Queen Elizabeth, have served England well. Today, as in the past, the sea directly provides large numbers of Englishmen with their livelihood. Fishing is carried on all around the coasts, some of the busiest ports being those along the East Coast—Yarmouth, Lowestoft and Grimsby. Millions of tons of food are won from the restless seas every year, and besides satisfying the demands at home it contributes to the export trade. The canning of fish like herrings and pilchards is a thriving modern industry which has given new importance to the fishing trade. England, though a tiny island, has some of the largest and best equipped commercial docks and harbours in the world. Shipbuilding employs nearly a quarter of a million men, chiefly in the great shipyards of the rivers Mersey, Humber, Tees and the Tyne.

FISHERMEN PREPARE FOR

Along the quayside at North Shields fishermen are getting their boats in shape again especially for the next trip to sea. North Shields is one of the busiest fishing ports

ANOTHER NIGHT'S WORK

of north-east England today, and especially during the herring season it is visited by numbers of drifters and trawlers making their contributions to the nation's larder.

FISHING FLEET

In the teeth of a biting north-easterly wind the Yarmouth herring drifters set their course at sundown for the lonely fishing grounds of the North Sea. Manned by crews of the sturdiest breed, these little ships stand up to the heavy seas and gales which are the common experience of the thousands of men who spend their lives fishing off

LEAVES PORT

the eastern shores of England. Herring fishing is a great industry on the East Coast where its chief centre is Great Yarmouth ; the season is at its height during the months of October and November, when many hundreds of drifters are working from the port. On the left two cheerful members of a drifter's crew are seen handling a good catch.

89

AT SEA AND IN PORT

A drifter's nets will often extend for two or three miles forming a vast barrier just below
the surface against which the fish are caught. Hauling in the nets (seen on the
right) is a laborious task. Sometimes accidents happen; the porpoise in the foreground
of the bottom picture at right tore the net. The quayside scene above is at Grimsby.

ON YARMOUTH QUAY

Because first ships in may command the best prices for their catch drifters often race one another to port. Unloading produces quayside scenes of orderly activity.

FISHER GIRLS AT WORK

Hundreds of Scottish fisher girls invade Yarmouth during the season. At shallow troughs along the quayside, they gut the herrings and salt them in readiness for export.

IN THE FISHING VILLAGES

Every village around the English coast is largely inhabited by the fisher-folk who carry on the trade of their ancestors. One or two boats are usually owned by each family, whose menfolk share the work and the profits from the fish caught. When the fishermen are not at sea they busy themselves with a variety of occupations linked with their trade. In the picture below a fisherman mends a lobster pot on the quay at Staithes, Yorkshire : top right, net-repairing on a Sussex beach : bottom right, boat-building at Porthleven.

The harbour at St. Ives, Cornwall

BUILDING THE SHIPS

Ship-building is one of England's oldest and most essential industries and, because of her long dependence on the sea, the nation owes a great debt to her shipyard workers. Nowadays ship-building combines a great number of trades and the shipyards, which have grown up along broad rivers like the Humber, the Mersey and the Tees are almost

IN ENGLISH YARDS

like towns laid out with factories, workshops and railways and planned for maximum efficiency. The workers, too, are all of them highly skilled craftsmen. New ocean going liners are seen under construction by night and by day in the Merseyside yards, and these pictures give some idea of the size and very great complexity of the task.

A NEW SHIP GOES

There is great excitement in the shipyard on the day that a new vessel is ready to take the water. The same detailed planning must precede the launching of any ship, whether it be an ordinary cargo vessel or a huge luxury liner, so that it is transferred

DOWN THE SLIPWAY

to the water without the slightest damage. The men who have helped to build her watch with pride as the new ship goes slowly down the slipways. Though the main task is finished, much work still remains to be done in fitting out and installing machinery.

TUGBOATS AND STEVEDORES

The docks and harbours around the coasts play a vital part in the national life, for much of our food and essential merchandise comes from overseas. The docks of the Port of London are the largest and most important in the world, containing a total water area of more than 700 acres and handling some 2,000,000 tons of cargo every month.

AT WORK IN THE DOCKS

Typical dockland scenes showing the loading and discharging of cargoes in the port are shown at left and right. Other big commercial docks are at Liverpool, Hull, Birkenhead, Manchester and Bristol. Southampton Docks (above centre) deal with the fast mail and passenger liners to America and contain the world's largest dry dock.

RELIEVING LIGHTHOUSE KEEPERS

Many lighthouses are in very exposed situations so that in rough weather the relief of those manning them is fraught with difficulties, some idea of which can be gathered from these photographs taken at the Bishop's Rock, above, and Longships lighthouses.

LIGHTHOUSES ROUND THE COASTS

The wonderful system of lighthouses, lightships and navigation buoys in operation round our shores helps materially to reduce the danger to shipping during bad weather. Since 1854 these installations have been under the supervision of Trinity House.

FISHING SMACKS RETURN WITH THE CATCH

These graceful yacht-like vessels, seen returning to port from the fishing grounds of the North Sea, form part of the fishing fleets that work from the villages along the estuaries of Essex. The Essex coast is broken by many long river estuaries, notably those of the Crouch, Blackwater and Colne, and ever since the days of the Romans they have been busy fishing centres. Most of the fishing vessels today make up the fairly numerous oyster-dredging fleet, and although Whitstable, in Kent, is the chief centre of Britain's oyster fisheries, there are also numerous very rich beds lying off the Essex shores.

LAUNCHING THE LIFEBOAT

England was the first country to have a lifeboat service, but despite the volume of maritime trade and the many dangers of the rock-bound coasts, it was not until 1780 that the first attempt was made to construct a suitable boat. Benevolent individuals by providing boats of their own at a few places provided the only attempts at organized life saving prior to 1824 in which year the Royal National Lifeboat Institution was formed. The volunteers who man the lifeboats have earned for themselves and the Institution a remarkable reputation for heroism and constant devotion to duty.

MEN AND SHIPS

The Royal Navy is the senior service of Britain with long and proud traditions. In peace-time its ships carry out many important functions on all the Seven Seas. On these pages are some of the men and the ships. At top (left to right) a Petty Officer

108

OF THE ROYAL NAVY

of the minesweeper service, a Signalman with an Aldis lamp, and H.M. the King, Admiral of the Fleet, inspecting the ship's company of H.M.S. Duke of York. Below (left to right) a meal in a submarine, dealing out rum; heavy seas break over H.M.S. Renown.

Holiday crowd at Waterloo Station

They serve the People

THE various public services of England today are run so very smoothly and efficiently that most people have come to take them for granted. The Englishman expects his trains to run to time, the letters he posts to distant towns to be delivered correctly by next morning, the police to uphold his rights of liberty, and so on. He expects these things because he has been used to them for so long. Nowadays the railways and local omnibuses, which serve even the remotest villages and hamlets, are augmented by an up-to-date airways system. Business men can travel between London and Manchester or Liverpool almost as quickly as they can drive across Greater London. The English countryside now has many of the benefits of modern civilisation; telephone and wireless keep even the most isolated farms in constant touch with life in the cities, and there are good medical and hospital services in every district. Many country-dwellers have the benefit of electric light and power in their homes, thanks to the grid system of electricity transmission. Roads, railways and canals share the burdens of commercial transport between the ports, factories, mines and farms.

III

THE RAILWAYS

A great network of railways serves the whole of England today and fast, comfortable express trains carry passengers from one end of the land to the other within five or six hours. England is the traditional home of the Iron Road for it was here that the first steam locomotive was invented and the first railway, the famous Stockton and Darlington line, was opened in 1825. Thereafter British railways developed rapidly until there were more than one hundred and twenty separate companies. These were amalgamated by an Act of Parliament which took effect in January 1923, when four big main companies emerged. They are the London, Midland and Scottish; the London and North Eastern; the Great Western, and the Southern Railways. Railways in Britain are justly proud of their records for speed, safety and comfort and first-class tracks made for smooth running. On the left two long-distance expresses leave Newcastle-on-Tyne. Above, the signalman on whose work safe travel so largely depends.

EASTWARD BOUND

The famous Cornish Riviera Express passing along the Devon coast en route from Penzance.
There are sea views between Dawlish and Teignmouth where the line runs on the coast.

READY FOR THE RUN

The express train drivers are highly skilled men with a lifetime of experience on the railways. This " Flying Scotsman " driver awaits the signal to start on another long trip.

BUILDING NEW LOCOMOTIVES

Each of the four big railway companies designs and builds its own locomotives and rolling stock. Inside the important Crewe works wheels are prepared for a new locomotive, while a completed engine is raised by travelling crane for transfer to the track.

RELAYING THE TRACK

Platelaying gangs work up and down the tracks, testing rails or relaying new ones. The railways consume nearly 250,000 tons of steel every year for the renewal of rails alone, and no time or money is spared to keep the permanent way in perfect condition.

LIFE ON THE CANALS

The canals still play a most useful part in the transport system of England. Forming a vast web of waterways throughout most of the country, they link the seaports and docks with the industrial towns and cities inland. Above, a string of barges is towed by a power barge on the Regent's Park Canal, part of the Grand Union Canal system. On the facing page, top, is a family of barge folk at Runcorn Lock on the Bridgewater Canal. Below, the living room mat is shaken overside and a pole is used to fend off from the bank.

THE POSTAL SERVICES

In the chain of distribution of mail the Post Office operates mail vans on long distance express trains and even an underground railway, but the real basis of fast postal service is the regular collections of which one is seen in progress on the facing page. For long distances in outlying districts, as at Clovelly above, pack animals are used.

THEY CARRY LONDON'S MILLIONS

Though largely replaced by trolley buses, trams still operate along the Thames Embankment and to some of the suburbs. The volume of traffic required to move London's millions is so very great that if even a small delay is caused to the flow on the roads, a big hold up of traffic, like the one at Marble Arch on the facing page, is caused.

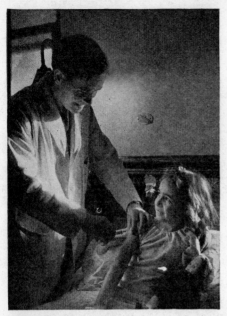

IN THE HOSPITALS

By day and by night the miraculous work of healing goes on all over England in the hospitals which are now among the best equipped in the world. The degree of skill among the doctors and nurses serving in the hospitals is also second to none. Today every town and city in the country has its hospital services and special clinics for the young, whose health is of paramount importance to the nation. Expert medical attention is also given in the schools and the factories, and each district has its local nursing services. Left, a doctor injecting a child with penicillin for her heart; below, in a ward of a naval hospital; right, surgeons at work in an operating theatre.

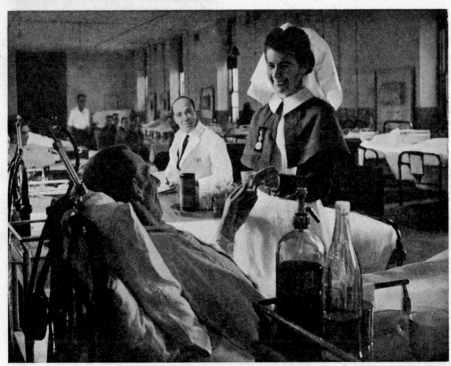

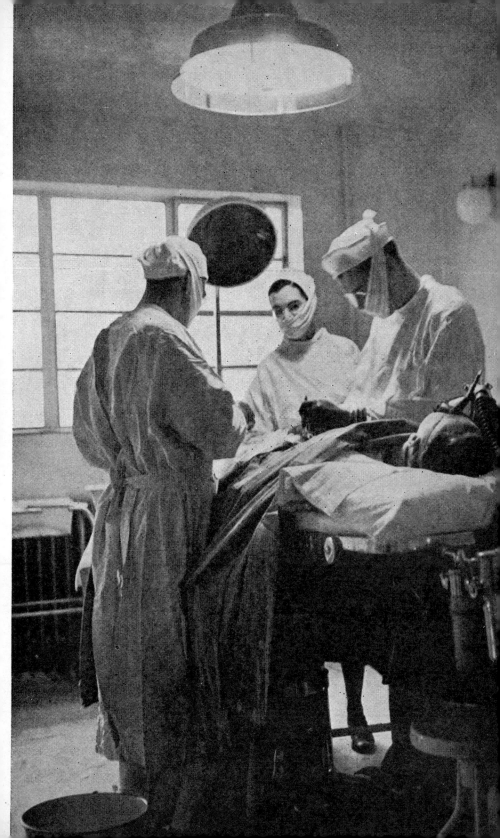

ENGLISH AIRWAYS

An up-to-date airways service covers the whole of the British Isles and all the largest cities of England have their airports. Passenger aeroplanes also link the Scillies and the Channel Islands with the mainland, and there is a daily service between London and various parts of the Continent. In addition, of course, there are regular air liner services covering practically the whole of the world. The Vickers Viking, seen above, is the latest short-distance air liner to be used on the European services of British Overseas Airways Corporation. Pilots give high praise to its performance. At right, passengers embark at Croydon, journeying from London by motor coach.

MAINTAINING LONDON'S UNDERGROUND SEWERS

Deep below London's streets run hundreds of miles of tunnels and pipes which carry 100,000 million gallons of sewage annually. Large maintenance staffs are employed.

GAS AND WATER SUPPLIES

Gas as an illuminant was first used in England about the beginning of the nineteenth century, chiefly through the discoveries made by William Murdock, the famous Cornish engineer. By 1815 the streets of London were being lit by gas, and Westminster Bridge and the Houses of Parliament were fitted for gas-burning. With the steady development of the gas industry, works sprang up in towns and cities all over the country and huge gas-holders became an ugly and permanent feature of urban landscapes. The picture above shows the large gasworks at Southall, on the outskirts of London. After the gas has been made it is stored in gas-holders, three of which are seen here at different stages of capacity. That in the foreground is quite full, while the one on the left is deflated, the supply having been used up by local consumers. Even more important to the community than gas is water, and England today can boast the best and the purest domestic water supplies in the world. Greater London gets its daily average of 300,000,000 gallons of water from the River Thames, the Lea Valley, in Hertfordshire, and wells close at hand. Birmingham's tap water, however, travels about eighty miles by pipeline from three great artificial lakes in the heart of Wales, while Manchester is chiefly supplied by Lake Thirlmere, in Cumberland, about ninety miles away. Fifty years ago the Liverpool City Council created the artificial Lake Vyrnwy, in North Wales, and built the largest dam in Europe to impound its waters to supply the needs of a huge city. The increasing demands for water supplies by growing towns and cities during the past half a century has resulted in several hundreds of square miles of England and Wales being deliberately flooded. Typical pumping engines are shown on the opposite page. These, at Sunbury, near London, are capable of pumping 16,000,000 gallons a day.

ELECTRIC LIGHT AND

A vast network of electric transmission lines now covers almost the whole of England, bringing light and power to towns, villages and farms. Huge modern power stations,

POWER SERVICES

like this one at Battersea beside the Thames in London, keep the Grid supplied and electricity is carried across the length and breadth of the country on tall steel pylons.

FIREMEN IN ACTION

Outbreaks of fire occur every day in densely populated cities and sometimes fire on the heath or in the farmer's stacks is sufficiently serious to require the National Fire Service, which is the most efficient body of its kind in the world and gets a serious fire under control in a very short time. Above, fighting a blaze in a Thames-side warehouse from a fire float on the river. These floats are used for all river-side and shipping fires. On the left firemen are seen clearing debris from a flooded courtyard after a factory fire in the Camberwell district. Opposite page, firemen in action during a serious blaze which gutted an office building in Barbican, near the Old Bailey in London. Through microphones fixed beside them the firemen on the ladders can communicate with the driver on the ground.

VARIED DUTIES OF

It is as traffic controllers that the police are seen most often by the ordinary citizen ; pointsmen are shown in the City of London, top left, and at Rochester in Kent, below. The picture at top right shows the good relations which exist between the citizen and the police, in this instance assisted in crowd control by another of His Majesty's servants,

THE POLICE FORCE

*a naval rating.   The earphones worn by the constable in the patrol car, bottom right,
show that he is in wireless communication with headquarters at New Scotland Yard.   In
the report room, bottom centre, constables receive reports from patrol cars by wireless
and from other sources by telephone.   Incidents are noted on large wall maps.*

BRIXTON ROAD, LONDON

The Englishman's Home

ALTHOUGH the English have won renown as seafarers and world explorers they are at heart a home-loving race. The desire of the average young Englishman is to have a house and a garden of his own where he can live with his family in the way he chooses and enjoy comfort and privacy. Above everything else, perhaps, he likes privacy. The people of this country have always taken great pride in their homes, however humble, and pleasure in cultivating their gardens. For hundreds of years the building of small homes, as well as large mansions, has been an important craft in England, nowhere better exemplified than in the villages. Many timber, stone and thatched cottages built as long ago as the Tudor period still add charm to English landscapes. These, together with the beautiful old manor houses built by noblemen through the ages, form part of the rich architectural legacy of England. In more recent times people have congregated in and about the towns where new blocks of workers' flats are gradually replacing the slum dwellings of the Victorian age. The town suburb, with its spacious avenues and gardens is a feature of present-day England.

137

LONDON CONTRASTS

The graceful Regency houses, top left, are in Belgrave Square, Westminster, which gave its name to one of the capital's most famous districts. This square was built in 1827-28 when John Nash, architect to the Prince Regent, was designing residential areas. Railed off in the centre is a garden which is reserved for the use of square residents, though in recent years, as a result of the tendency to convert the houses into offices, many of these gardens have been redesigned as public open spaces. Quite often the mansions of the wealthiest citizens are but a short distance from the homes of the poor. The roofs and chimneys, bottom left, are of Victorian tenement buildings near St. Pancras Station ; ugly, dingy and overcrowded, they add only drabness to the London scene and provide a striking contrast to the well designed and comparatively spacious houses shown above in a modern residential road in the suburban district of Worcester Park. The semi-detached houses have each their tiny plot before the front door and a larger garden at the back ; amenities of especial value when there are children in the family. The enclosed garden of the wealthy and the absence of garden for the poor are alike of the past ; the tendency now is for each building to have its own private garden.

IN LONDON'S EAST END

Slum areas of London and other great cities where many of the community have to spend most of their lives, are a grim legacy of Victorian England, when, in the decades following the Industrial Revolution, mile after mile of mean and dingy streets flanked by tenement houses grew up in the rapidly developing cities like Liverpool, Manchester, Birmingham and Newcastle-on-Tyne. In such surroundings hundreds of thousands of children grow up seeing little of green grass or blue sky. Though such living conditions still remain a large, ugly blot on the face of English cities, and it will be many years before the last of them disappears, they are gradually being swept away.

STREETS OF TOWN AND VILLAGE

The street above, which is in South London, is typical of many hundreds throughout the Metropolis ; its drab uniformity marks town and suburban housing of the late nineteenth century. Though once there were open spaces near at hand, now shops, factories and warehouses encroach on almost every yard of ground. These houses have no gardens and only small backyards, so that children must face the hazards of play in the roadway. By contrast the quaint old main street at Lynmouth in Devon, top left on the facing page, though its houses crowd closely on one another as the street climbs from the harbour, from that very fact derives a charm which it can never lose. The lack of free space is of no consequence in a small town with open country close even to its centre. At Chipping Campden, bottom left, one of the loveliest little towns of the Cotswold country of Gloucestershire, the dignified and gabled houses were built by citizens many of whom were prosperous wool merchants, for the town was formerly a busy centre of the local wool trade. Today it is important as a market town for the surrounding farms and is a popular resort for those who like a holiday in the country. The peach-coloured stone which is quarried locally gives lasting beauty to Cotswold architecture.

Buckland in the Moor, Devonshire

A KENTISH HOME

In the village of Lenham near Maidstone, this fine half-timbered house has been standing for more than three hundred years. This is a favourite style of building in south-eastern England where the wooded valleys and hillsides provided much excellent timber.

146

A COTTAGE IN WILTSHIRE

The well-thatched roof of a cosy cottage in Castle Combe, a favourite Wiltshire beauty spot, comes down over the eaves to give protection against storms and gales. It keeps the house warm and dry in winter and cool in summer. Thatching is a highly skilled craft.

HOMES OF THE COUNTRY

Homes both palatial and humble are to be found in great variety around the countryside of England. In almost every county the materials and methods of using them are different and the resulting styles of old houses and cottages add much to the natural charm of the varied landscapes. On the left-hand page are two distinct cottage styles. Above, a row of fishermen's dwellings at Sheringham on the Norfolk coast, where the walls are faced with the same cobblestones which made the narrow roadway outside. The cottage shown below stands at Smarden in Kent, and the weatherboarding which covers its walls is a style favoured by the local building craftsmen. Interesting contrast is provided with a view of Charlecote House near Stratford-on-Avon, one of the famous old Elizabethan mansions and ancestral home of the Lucy family. Built of Cotswold stone, Charlecote House is surrounded by a finely wooded deer-park through which the Avon flows and it was here that the youthful Shakespeare was once caught stealing deer.

FARM IN THE CHILTERN HILLS

MEVAGISSEY IN CORNWALL

Fishermen's cottages cluster above the busy little harbour of one of the picturesque villages along the Cornish coast. These homes are all built of the hard local granite.

CLOVELLY IN DEVON

Built on a cliff side with a steep main street descending by steps to the harbour, this is one of the best-known fishing villages of North Devon. Donkey transport is used.

THE HOUSEWIFE'S CHANGING DEMESNE

In the kitchen of the old inn in Saltergate in Yorkshire, top on facing page, the peat fire never goes out and the oven is used daily to bake bread. A lump of peat fuel is seen on the hearth. Though less picturesque, the modern kitchen of the suburban home in Northolt, shown beneath, is better for the housewife since it is designed to save labour. The water-heater, well-placed cupboards and drawers and the modern cooking stove are both more convenient and more economic to operate than the old-fashioned ranges. The farmer, his family and land girls, above, live in a well-built modern house in the Home Counties showing that advance in domestic architecture is not confined to the cities.

OLD PEOPLE AT HOME

This old couple enjoy the modest comfort of their home in an older suburb of London.
The room is furnished in late Victorian style, fashionable at the time of their marriage.

IN AN OLD FARMSTEAD

A Cumberland farmer and his two sons enjoy a rest by the fireside after the midday meal before returning to their work in the fields. Even to the hardened mountain farmer the climbing of the steep fells to look after the sheep taxes the energy and an afternoon siesta is well earned. This picture is typical of an old English farm house in which the kitchen is generally used as the chief living room. The old rocking-chair in which the farmer sits was probably used by his grandfather and great grandfather and has stood by the same fireside through all the years. Great flitches of home-cured bacon hang from hooks on the ceiling and nearby there will be a larder well stocked with all the good things grown and produced on this farm which is situated close to Lake Buttermere.

HOMES OF THE PEOPLE

At the top of the facing page a North Country miner, squatting, as do all miners, to relieve his stomach muscles after long hours of crouching and crawling, enjoys a quiet smoke by his own fireside while waiting for the bath which he takes before his supper. Below, a family is spending the evening in a pleasant living room typical of thousands in which live the black-coated workers of the middle class. Above is a fine block of working-class flats in Liverpool, following the design of very many others which have been built in the great industrial centres. Such buildings provide light, airy and well-equipped homes in which, while the housewife has the advantage of modern labour-saving conveniences, her children play safely in the surrounding courtyards and gardens.

Sheep from the Mendip Hills

BISHOP'S STORTFORD

Life in Town and Country

WHILE great changes have come about in the larger towns and cities within the last century, the people of the villages and remoter hamlets and farms still follow much the same ways of life as their ancestors have done through the ages. The English countryman leads a simple hard-working life and his close relationship with the soil makes him happy and contented. The older market towns all over the country have a charm of their own, many of them preserving a medieval atmosphere; weekly market days and the annual fairs bring liveliness to their streets. Life in the greater cities all over the world follows a rather similar pattern, but in those of England the old traditions and civic customs survive, to impress under the pattern of modern industry a character at once dignified and very colourful, dear to the hearts of the English people. Most big provincial centres today offer services and entertainments comparable with those of London itself, even if the glamour of the capital be missing. In the country no less than in the town there is the English inn, a peculiar national institution, where sooner or later one may meet most of the people who live in town and country.

SHOPPING SCENES

Shopping, part of every housewife's daily routine, can be done in very different surroundings. Above, an old-fashioned village shop at Lenham, in Kent, where a country housewife goes shopping with the aid of her bicycle. Very different is the bustle of a crowded city market. Berwick market, top right, is a flourishing centre of Cockney street traders only a stone's throw from Piccadilly Circus. Below, Sunday morning in Middlesex Street, better known as Petticoat Lane, one of London's markets.

Market Day at Romford, Essex

MARKETS IN TOWN AND VILLAGE

Down in West Somerset the little village of Porlock has its weekly market, top left, where locally grown vegetables, fruit and flowers are sold direct to the villagers, as was the practice everywhere in days gone by. Many of these village produce-centres have been revived in the past few years. The local markets, of course, went into the towns when these as time went on grew up. Today they survive, often in the form of groups of street traders, one of whom is doing a brisk business below in a shopping centre of Sheffield. The increase of town populations outgrew the local markets and resulted in the development of the great central distribution centres of which Covent Garden is London's principal market for fruit, flowers and vegetables. This market, the largest of its kind in the world, was founded in the reign of King Charles II. Scenes similar to that above are to be witnessed there early on any normal weekday morning.

SHOP WINDOW ATTRACTIONS

Shop-gazing is one of life's simple pleasures and every town, big or small, ancient or modern, offers windows in endless variety. Youngsters on the left are attracted by the wares in a small store in the old-world city of Shrewsbury. More modern displays draw attention to the stores in Oxford Street in London's fashionable shopping district.

IN HIGHGATE WOODS

London's beautiful parks and open spaces bring a breath of the countryside into the heart of the capital. The charming scene above is in Highgate Woods, North London.

THE LAKE IN REGENT'S PARK

A peaceful spring evening on the lake in Regent's Park, which also has other attractions for Londoners in its pleasant avenues and, in summer, its beds of glorious flowers.

Midday in St. James's Park

ORATORS' CORNER AT

Every evening and at week-ends crowds gather in that corner of Hyde Park facing
the Marble Arch to listen to the speakers. Here orators from every walk of life declaim
on any and every conceivable subject from religion to dog racing. Politics and religion

HYDE PARK, LONDON

are the favourite topics ; sometimes as many as twenty meetings may be in progress at once. A section of the enormous crowd round the rostrums is shown above with some of the speakers' expressions. One of the audience, bottom right, listens intently.

LEISURE HOURS AT THE INN

The old inns of town and village have played an important part in the life of England for many centuries and they still do so today. The English inn is something much more than an ordinary drinking house. In most places it is a local centre of social life ; in the public bar or the saloon men of all classes meet after the day's work is over to enjoy pleasant discussion or a game of darts or dominoes in good companionship and comfortable surroundings. In the bar parlour of an old village inn of the West Country, above, some of the local inhabitants gather round the skittles, one of the traditional public house games of England. Over a glass of ale they discuss the news of the day. This low-ceilinged room has hardly changed at all since the inn was built some two hundred years ago. Top right, a group of Midland colliery workers get together round the table in their local inn for the favourite nightly game of dominoes. Below, guests receiving drinks from their hostess in the saloon bar of the old Swan Inn at West Wycombe—a charming example of a sixteenth century hostelry.

ENGLISH WEDDINGS

Everybody loves a wedding, especially a church wedding. The English, like many other peoples, make the most of such ceremonies. Above, after a village church wedding the bride and bridegroom leave in an old-fashioned horse trap. Top right, a society wedding at St. Margaret's, Westminster. Below, a lively wedding scene in the East End of London.

Regent Street, in the heart of London's West End, is typical of the busy shopping thoroughfares of the metropolis. The ever-changing pageant of the crowds and the traffic help to make up the irresistible charm of the greatest city in the world. Shown, too, are some of the characters and tradesmen seen in the streets of London and its

LONDON'S STREETS

suburban districts. The shoe-black and the knife-grinder are among the oldest of the city's one-man trades and their services are still in great demand. The lamp-lighter is less familiar in these days of electricity, but he is still kept busy cleaning lamps. Coal delivery and refuse collection are occupations which remain essential services.

AT THE FAIR

Summer fairs are held in towns and villages all over England, and at Pinner, Middlesex, the roundabouts and various amusement booths are set up in the High Street. Pearly kings and queens are familiar characters at the fairgrounds around London; the picture at top right shows a family at the famous fair held on August Bank Holiday on Hampstead Heath. Gipsies follow the fairs around, too. Bottom right, a typical gipsy camp.

MAIN ROAD IN THE CITY OF LONDON

*The great volume of traffic which flows through the narrow streets of the City is shown
by these weekday streams converging from Queen Victoria Street, left, and Cannon Street.*

186

MAIN ROAD IN A VILLAGE OF KENT

The High Street is the main thoroughfare of Brenchley. Through it cows pass at leisurely gait, providing striking contrast with the normal traffic of a weekday in London.

ON ENGLISH ROADS

The winding roads and lanes of England are among the charms of the countryside although many of them have become unsuited to present-day traffic conditions. In recent years, however, great new arterial highways and wide by-pass roads around the towns and cities have been constructed, and the pictures on these pages show contrast between the new and the old. On weekdays and at night-time heavy lorries and other transport vehicles are much in evidence, and the roadside cafes are patronized by the good-humoured drivers. But at week-ends, especially during the summer months, the roads are thronged with motorists and cyclists from the towns seeking the joys of countryside and coast. Pictures were taken at Boxhill in Surrey, right, and the Hog's Back, above.

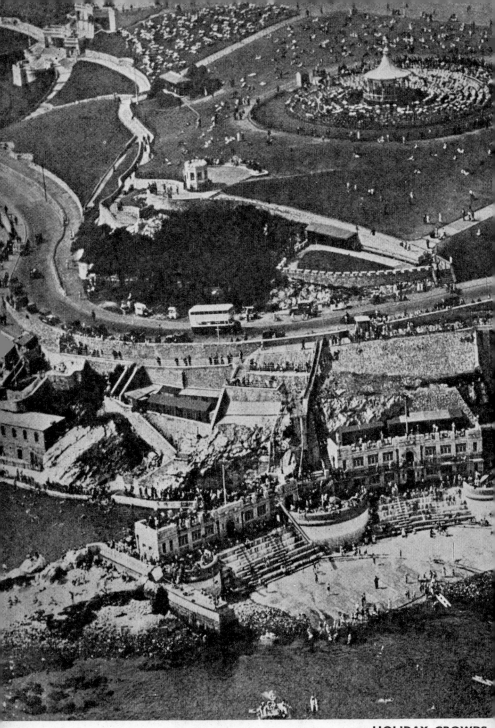

HOLIDAY CROWDS

Today the foremost port of Elizabethan times manufactures soap, chemicals and electrical goods. It is still a naval base and important commercial harbour, and in

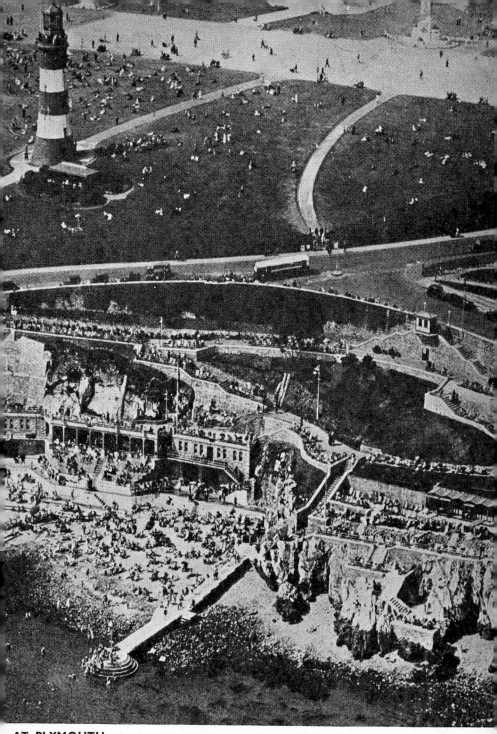

AT PLYMOUTH

summer its beaches attract large holiday crowds. The historic greensward and the
ornamental gardens now on Plymouth Hoe stretch inland from the cliffs shown above.

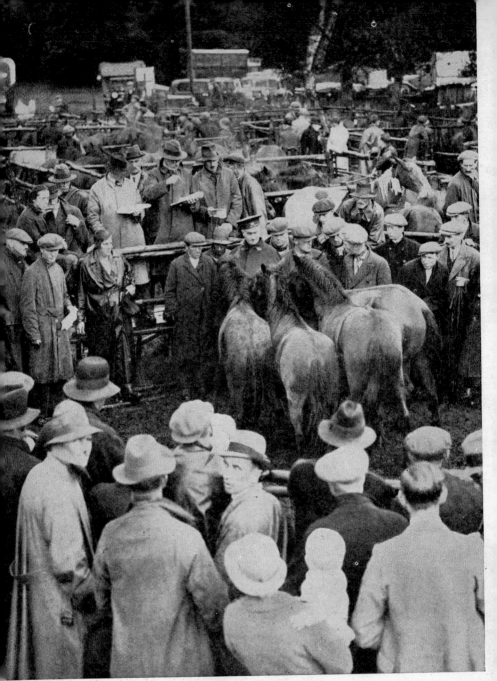

FOREST PONY SALE

The New Forest in Hampshire is one of the few woodland areas left in England; it was one of the five forests listed in Domesday and in it ponies have run wild ever since Saxon times. Anyone who owns any of the ponies has to pay a small annual rent to the Crown. Once a year the older ponies are rounded up and sold by auction. Some go to distant collieries, others to serve the local farmers and tradesmen. This sale is near Beaulieu.

ENGLISH ZOOLOGICAL GARDENS

One of the most famous collections of wild and rare animals is housed in the Gardens of the Zoological Society in Regent's Park, London. Founded in 1828 the London Zoo attracts hundreds of thousands of visitors a year. Children are seen enjoying elephant rides (top). Other towns have their own zoological gardens too. Below, left, a lioness and cubs at the Bristol Zoo; right, the polar bear pit at Dudley Zoo, in Worcestershire.

VILLAGE LIFE IN ENGLAND

This beautiful row of cottage homes is a corner of the famous village of Bibury, in Gloucestershire, and is typical of the domestic architecture of the Cotswold country. Nowadays the village folk of England enjoy many amenities of civilization denied to them in the past. Top, right, railwaymen playing a game of dominoes in the recreation room of a country workers' hostel. Below, serving hot meals to aged folk in a village canteen.

THAMES LIGHTERS AT KEW

The large flat-bottomed lighter, commonly but less properly known as a barge, plays a very important part in the operation of the London Docks. Cargoes brought in ocean-going vessels can be unloaded into lighters and then, as with this timber seen at Kew on its way up river, taken by a most economical form of transport to riverside storage.

SAILING BARGES ON THE THAMES

Sailing barges such as these at anchor off Woolwich are used mainly for river and coastal trade but also travel as far afield as Holland, Belgium, the Channel Islands and France. For river work they are usually between 80 and 180 tons' burden but coastal craft may be up to 300 tons. These shallow-draft vessels require a crew of no more than four.

LIFE IN THE FIELDS

Working life on the farms of England provides many such attractive and contrasting scenes as those reproduced on these pages. The picture above was taken on a farm near Brightlingsea, in Essex, where harvested oats are being loaded on to an old-style horse wagon. The rich heavy soils of Essex make the county particularly suitable for the extensive cultivation of grain crops like oats and wheat. Right, a familiar ploughing scene on a fell farm at Threlkeld, in Cumberland. It is early spring and the mountain peaks seen in the background, part of the famous Skiddaw range, are covered with snow.

ST. EWE, CORNWALL

EAST ANGLIAN PLOUGHMAN

*After the midday break this Suffolk ploughman leads his pair of horses back to the
fields on a farm near Sudbury. Suffolk is predominantly a county of arable land where
a variety of crops is grown and most of the soil is brought under the plough year after
year. Much wheat and barley is gathered as well as sugar beet, potatoes and flax.*

HILLS AND RIVERS OF THE SOUTH

Kent is a county well loved by walkers and cyclists. The picture above was taken on the summit of Ide Hill, near Sevenoaks, a favourite beauty spot commanding extensive views across the Weald. Below, on the waterways of Essex, a sailing barge passes by the town of Wivenhoe, near Colchester, on its way down the estuary of the River Colne.

BRINGING BRACKEN TO THE FARM

A load of bracken, which is used primarily as bedding for cattle, for thatching and sometimes for fodder, is brought into the village of Albury, Surrey. This is one of the charming little villages which lie in a wooded valley under the slopes of the North Downs between Dorking and Guildford. The houses shown date from the seventeenth century.

TRADE ON THE SOUTH COAST

Many and varied activities are carried on by inhabitants in the small ports and fishing harbours along the Channel coast of England. The top picture shows a cargo of Finnish timber being unloaded on the quayside at West Bay, Dorset, which is one of England's smallest ports. Below, keddle net fishermen unloading mackerel in Rye Bay, Sussex.

ON NORFOLK MARSH AND BROAD

*Great stretches of water and marshland cover the flat Norfolk countryside. Above, men
are gathering reeds by boat near Downham Market. These are used for thatching and
basket making. The Broads around Wroxham are still a paradise of the wild-fowler as
well as the yachtsman, and the picture below shows a duck-shoot on Ranworth Broad.*

CHARCOAL-BURNING

Charcoal-burning is one of the ancient country crafts of Britain. This picture from the Forest of Dean shows a burner preparing his " pile." Thousands of logs form the mound, a central chimney being left for the fire. The mound is covered with turf or dry bracken and allowed to smoulder for days until the wood is thoroughly charred.

Open Air Theatre, Regent's Park, London

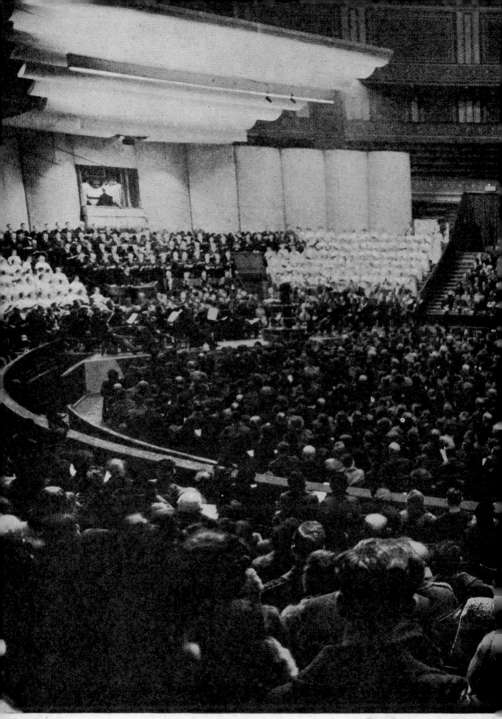

CONCERT AT THE

London is the musical centre of England and all through the year a great variety of concerts and recitals are performed by the world's finest orchestras and the most famous

ROYAL ALBERT HALL

artists. *The Royal Albert Hall, scene of the famous " Proms," is here filled to capacity for a performance of Beethoven's Solemn Mass by the Huddersfield Choral Society.*

ROYAL MILITARY TATTOO

One of the most spectacular outdoor entertainments in England is the Aldershot Tattoo
which takes place every June and draws huge crowds. In a huge arena a series of
exciting and colourful tableaux are presented in which many thousand soldiers take a

AT RUSHMERE ARENA, ALDERSHOT

*part, including the finest massed bands of the British Army.   The varied scenes cover
many famous events of English history from the time of the Norman conquest to the
present.   Here an afternoon rehearsal of the tattoo is watched by thousands of children.*

Football Cup Final at Wembley Stadium

England at Play

NO nation enjoys so many kinds of sport as the English, whose love of games has so often been derided by the serious minded. The most popular game of the winter is football, played everywhere and attractive to millions of spectators. In the summer, as is natural for an island people, there are rowing, yachting and swimming, but it cannot be said that their following is so large as those of some other activities. Wide popular interest centres on cricket, for which Lord's ground is a popular point of focus, and lawn tennis, now perhaps more widely played than any game in the world and having its best known event in the championships at Wimbledon. All the year round there is racing of one kind or another, horse-racing leading in popularity, with events like the Derby and the Grand National world-famous. But it is not as sportsmen only that the English play. Many thousands find enjoyment less in organized games than in more personal pursuits, touring the countryside by cycle or by car or rambling through it on foot, sometimes staying away from home at an inn, a youth hostel or under canvas. While a few seek interest exploring the caverns of the Mendips, a multitude finds pleasure on the dance floor. Alone or in company most English men and women take delight either in the prowess of others or individually in the many varied sports and pastimes.

FOOTBALL

Football in England is played under three codes, Association, Rugby Union and Rugby League. As cricket is the great national game of the summer, so Association is the national game of the winter ; moreover, it has proved one of the most popular of English exports and now is played not merely among immediate neighbours on the Continent but as widely afield as South America, Africa, India and Russia. Rugby Union, played by fifteen men a side, is predominantly a game for amateurs made famous by the annual international contest between England, Ireland, Scotland, Wales and France. Rugby League football is played by teams of thirteen a side, is very similar in character to the Rugby Union game, but is played mainly in the north country by professional teams. Both codes of Rugby football have large and enthusiastic followings, but great as these are they bear no comparison with the crowds of hundreds of thousands which, week by week, throughout the winter, follow the fortunes of the professional " Soccer " teams up and down the country. In addition many thousands more are engaged each week in playing for the amateur teams of every efficiency which meet in keen rivalry in practically every town, village and hamlet. Above, in a Rugby Union game a successful place kick at goal has been made following a " try " and the successful side adds five points to its score, three for the try and two for the goal kick. On the facing page are scenes from Association football ; above, a tussle for the ball ; below, a goal is scored.

POPULAR SPORTS

Stick games have been played since ancient times and by many peoples, including the Red Indians of America, the ancient Persians, Greeks and Romans. The game of hockey as we know it, top on facing page, dates, however, only from 1875. Owing to very strict control this is one of the few games which has remained a sport played by amateurs only. Greyhound racing, below, was tried first at the Welsh Harp, Hendon, in 1876, but aroused no great enthusiasm in face of the opposition of those interested in coursing. Later, after gaining widespread popularity in America, the racing of greyhounds after a dummy hare was introduced to England in 1926 when a track was opened at Manchester. There are now regular meetings throughout the year at many of the big cities. Above is the ring at the Queensberry Club which takes its name from the eighth Marquess of Queensberry who, in conjunction with John Chambers, founder in 1866 of the Amateur Athletic Club, drew up the rules bearing his name which still control boxing in England. The introduction in the eighteenth century of boxing with gloves instead of bare knuckles is attributed to Jack Broughton, known as the father of British pugilism.

PLAY ON THE GREEN

Golf is one of the very few games which can be enjoyed alone and there is no other out-door sport in which the player's mistakes react so directly. Though the golfer can play at a speed to suit himself, attainment of the front rank demands stamina no less than

IN A GOLF MATCH

skill. So it is that for beginner and expert alike the game has great fascination. As the large gallery following play in a match on the Purley Downs Links in Surrey shows, struggles between leading golfers provide entertainment which is eagerly witnessed.

INDOOR SPORTS

Above, the table tennis championships are being contested. Though this game originated as a pastime on the dining table in the sedate atmosphere of Victorian family life it has been developed into a game for which a good deal of space and both agility and skill are needed. Badminton, pictured on the facing page, is another game extremely popular in winter. It usually is played in small halls as the necessary space and height are not found easily elsewhere. It can be played in the open air, but then wind introduces an element of chance which tends to spoil the game for the skilled player.

FOX-HUNTING IN

On a bright winter morning the South Berkshire Meet, led by huntsmen in the traditional
scarlet coats, moves off at a steady pace to the hunting field at School Green, near

THE ENGLISH COUNTRYSIDE

Reading. Fox-hunting is a favourite sport of the countryman, the season beginning in November. Many counties have famous hunting packs in charge of a Master of Hounds.

HORSE RACING

The origin of " the sport of Kings " is lost in antiquity. In England an Act of Parliament regulating the weights to be carried by racehorses was passed in 1740 and the Jockey Club, to the integrity of which is largely due the great growth of " the Turf," was formed about ten years later. Hurdle racing and steeplechasing, in which jumping obstacles forms part of the race, take place generally from November to March, and flat racing during the remainder of the year. At the top of the facing page horses are seen clearing Becher's Brook, one of the most famous jumps of the Grand National, a steeplechase, dating from 1839, run at Aintree near Liverpool. It is the support of the betting man, the " punter," which makes racing possible. A section of the crowd and the bookmakers at Ascot is shown below. The Betting Act of 1928 authorized the Jockey Club and National Hunt Committee to install the Totalisator ; a percentage of the money taken in bets is used for course maintenance and the payment of the stewards, as is the money paid by the " bookie " for his " stand " on the course. Above is a general view, which was taken from Trundle Hill, of the Course at Goodwood in Sussex.

RACING AT

The history of racing in England is for all intents and purposes the story of racing on Newmarket Heath. On this famous course, headquarters since 1750 of the Jockey

NEWMARKET

Club, are run the Cesarewitch and Cambridgeshire handicaps as well as the race for the Two Thousand Guineas, one of the five classic events of the Racing Calendar.

BATHING BEACH IN LONDON

A riverside beach in the heart of the City offers these young Londoners many of the joys of the seaside and their parents' relief from crowded streets. A scene on Tower Beach.

BATHING BEACH IN DEVON

Salterton Cove, near Paignton, is one of the delightful inlets around the rocky shores of Tor Bay in South Devon, where holiday-makers can enjoy secluded sun and sea bathing.

HOLIDAY CROWDS ON

In the eleventh century Brighton was a large fishing village. In the middle of the
eighteenth century its character changed and it came to be regarded as a fashionable
resort, of which the popularity was increased by the patronage in the 1780's of the

BRIGHTON BEACH

Prince of Wales. Today, though there are still mackerel and herring fisheries, Brighton is best known as one of the principal holiday resorts on the south coast. Electric trains can reach London in one hour, so that many business men have their homes there.

ROWING

Bumping races, like that shown above, originated early in the nineteenth century from the custom of the crews of eight-oared boats from Oxford racing one another on being released from Iffley Lock. A boat making a bump takes precedence over the one bumped in the order for the next day's racing. Perhaps the most famous of all rowing contests are those at the annual regatta held on the Thames at Henley, below.

YACHT RACING

*During the summer many exciting yacht racing contests are held around the coasts,
especially at the famous annual regattas at Cowes, Isle of Wight, and in Tor Bay, Devon.*

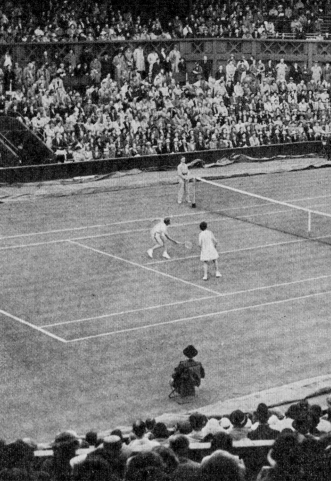

LAWN TENNIS, THE GAME MOST

In 1877 the real basis of the modern game of Lawn Tennis was laid by the committee
of the All England Club, until then devoted to croquet. The first championship meeting

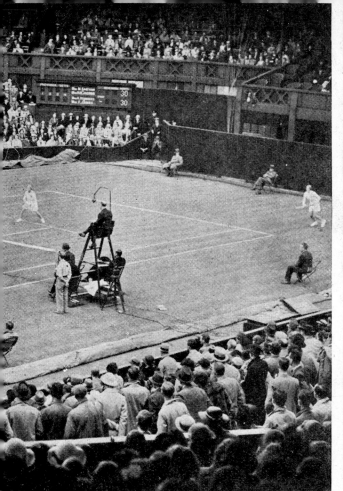

WIDELY PLAYED IN THE WORLD

was held in that year at Wimbledon. A match on the famous centre court is shown above, together with some studies in expression by individual players, expert and otherwise.

SUMMER PASTIMES

On a hot afternoon the peace of smooth-flowing water has a fascination which can lure any holiday maker. The scene above was taken on the Thames towpath near Richmond. The hiker, top right, pauses to study his map and the view before continuing his ramble through England's pleasant land. Bowls, played since the thirteenth century, is one of the oldest outdoor games, and good play requires skill. The green on which it is played may be either level or crown, which latter has a slight outward slope in all directions from the centre and is found mainly in the northern and midland counties.

ATHLETICS

Rivalry between the London Athletic Club, founded in 1863 by business men of Mincing Lane, and the Amateur Athletic Club, which started in 1866, led in 1879 to dual English Championship meetings. Next year the Amateur Athletic Association was formed and ever since has controlled athletics in England. Left : High jump competitor at an A.A.A. meeting. Below : Long jump at the public schools meeting held each year, inaugurated by the Achilles Club.

BALLROOM DANCING

Beside having a most important place in the social life of all sections of the community ballroom dancing provides healthy exercise, for all except the very young and very old.

241

MOTORING FOR PLEASURE

Main arteries of traffic cannot attract the motorist bent on pleasure, but for those with the leisure to explore the network of roads winding through the countryside there is a vast store of pleasant places to be visited. This party is at Godshill in the Isle of Wight.

THE SOCIAL SIDE OF CYCLING

In addition to the Cyclists Touring Club and National Cyclists Union, there are thousands of cycling clubs which provide both companionship on the road and a field of social activity for those with interests in the countryside. Above : A club party on the road.

Outdoor holidays have become much more popular in recent years, especially with the development of the trailer caravan which can be hitched on to the rear of a motor car.

LAKE DISTRICT

The English Lake District is a favourite choice for holidays of this kind, and above is an attractive camping site near Ambleside, on the east shore of Lake Windermere.

CYCLE RACING

Both road and track cycling have a following but cannot be regarded as popular sports in the sense that are cricket, tennis and football. In most countries there are national bodies which govern racing and these are bound together by the Union Cycliste Internationale which promotes and legislates for racing in all parts of the world. The race shown in the above picture is taking place on the famous track at Herne Hill.

246

BEAGLING

The Christ Church Beagles moving off from Denton near Oxford. There is excellent sport for a winter's morning following the hounds on foot as the pack hunts the hare.

POT-HOLING IN SOMERSET

A party of young cave-explorers refresh themselves after scrambling through half a mile of underground passages to reach Swildon's Hole, one of the most beautiful Mendip caves.

CRICKET MATCH ON

The village green at Chipperfield is one of the oldest cricket grounds in England. A match there, typical English cricket at its best, was described for listeners in America

THE VILLAGE GREEN

in the " People to People " series of the B.B.C. The delightful surroundings please the eye
and the inn provides an attractive locale for talking over the day's deeds after the match.

TOWER OF LONDON

English Pageantry

ANCIENT customs and traditions still play an important part in the everyday life of the English people. They govern the working of the supreme legislative assembly, the Houses of Parliament, and they are woven into the administration of the common laws of the land and local government. In towns and villages all over the country a great number of picturesque customs are revived year by year, particularly at such festivals of the Church as Eastertide and Christmas. Many other quaint ceremonies, such as those associated with May Day and Midsummer, are of remote pagan origin and have been handed down from forgotten times. Then there are the customs centred around the annual Harvest Festival which mark the great climax of the farmers' year. In the capital city of London the visitor may witness a host of characteristic English customs some of which, like the Ceremony of the Keys at the Tower, go on every day of the year. Among the annual ceremonies none arouses greater interest than the Lord Mayor's Show. The English are very proud of their wealth of traditions, and rightly so; for this forms a most interesting and colourful part of the nation's social heritage.

TROOPING THE COLOUR

MOUNTING GUARD AT BUCKINGHAM PALACE

The sentry guards on duty outside Buckingham Palace lend a touch of pageantry to
London all through the year. When the King is in residence the ceremony of Changing
the Guard takes place, the old guard marching to barracks behind the regimental band.

PAGEANTRY IN LONDON

Every night at the Tower of London, when the warders lock the gates, the historic ceremony of the King's Keys takes place. Picture above shows the escort being challenged with the question " Whose Keys ? " to which the answer is given " King George's Keys." Below, old Army pensioners on parade at Chelsea Hospital.

PROCESSION OF JUDGES

Every year in the autumn, at the opening of the Michaelmas Term of law sittings in
London, the judges, wearing their robes of office of the King's Bench and Court of Common

AT WESTMINSTER

Pleas, lead a procession to attend Divine service at Westminster Abbey. Afterwards, as shown above, they file into the House of Lords to take luncheon with the Lord Chancellor.

BEATING THE BOUNDS

The ceremony of Beating the Bounds is a survival from the Middle Ages when officials of every town and parish in England were charged with the duty of perambulating the boundaries once a year. Certain landmarks were beaten with long canes. London choirboys still perform at Temple Steps, St. Clement Danes (above), and around the Tower.

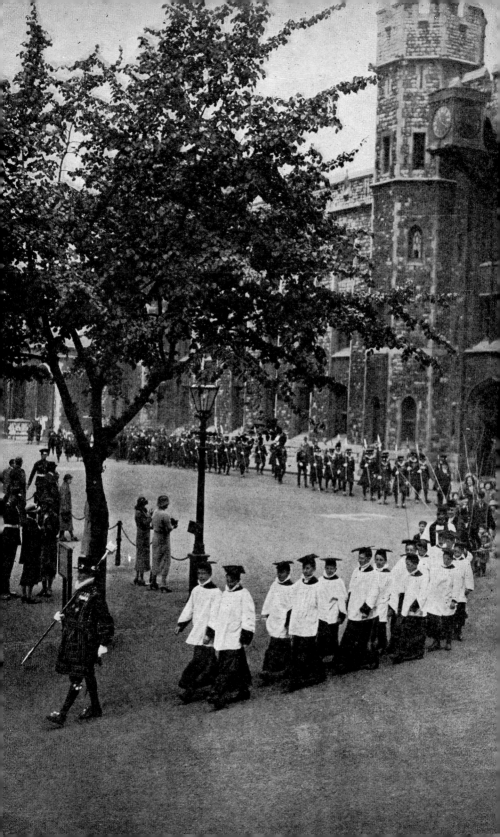

LORD MAYOR'S SHOW

The most spectacular of all London's old customs is the Lord Mayor's Show, which takes place on November 9th each year. The busy traffic of the capital has to be diverted from several important thoroughfares during the morning while the great procession, headed by the Lord Mayor's horse-drawn coach, wends its way from Guildhall to Temple Bar, one of the old city boundaries, and back to the Mansion House. The procession is a very colourful affair, resplendent with military uniforms and decorative tableaux which are carried on carts, and it never fails to attract large crowds of spectators.

WASSAILING IN DEVON

Every New Year's Eve the Devonshire farmers and their men go a-wassailing in the apple orchards. Trees are toasted in cider to ensure good crops for the following season and a shot is fired through their branches to drive away evil spirits. Wassail was the ancient form of toasting and became customary in lay houses and monasteries.

SHROVE TUESDAY CUSTOMS

One of the liveliest of the ancient Shrovetide customs is a communal football game in which an unlimited number of players take part. Below, the game in progress at Alnwick, Northumberland. The teams, representing the two local parishes, receive a new football for the occasion from the lodge of Alnwick Castle, seat of the Duke of Northumberland, and after a mad scramble the ball is kicked into the river. The first player to reach it is allowed to retain it as a souvenir. Above, housewives of Olney, Buckinghamshire, tossing their pancakes outside the church door after the Shrove Tuesday Pancake Race ; a local custom which has been observed for five hundred years.

EASTER CUSTOMS

At Easter the distribution of the Royal Maundy (top left) still takes place in Westminster Abbey, when as many aged men and women as there are years in the King's age receive specially minted silver pieces. Choirboys of St. Michael's Church, Bristol (bottom left) receive large buns, called Twopenny Starvers, on Easter Tuesday—a custom dating from the days when poor people could get only black bread and this occasion gave them one meal of white bread a year. The Pace-Eggers at Midgley, Yorkshire (above), give an old mumming play each Good Friday. Right, parishioners at Biddenden, in Kent, receiving their Easter dole of bread and a special biscuit—a custom which has been carried on for eight hundred years.

CONTRASTS IN ENGLISH PAGEANTRY

The dignity of the Yeomen of the Guard, seen marching to church at the Tower of London, makes strange contrast with a group of Coconut dancers above, performing their weird rites in a street at Bacup, Lancashire. But both are typical examples of our surviving English pageantry. The Yeomen of the Guard are a very ancient body, founded in the year 1485 to act as a personal bodyguard to the reigning Sovereign of England. To-day they number about one hundred men, all of them old soldiers with a distinguished record of service to their country, and their duties are purely ceremonial. One of these duties is a search of the vaults below the Houses of Parliament on the eve of the State opening. The Coconut dancers are miners who dance every Easter Monday.

HOCKTIDE AT HUNGERFORD

*On the Tuesday in the week following Easter the annual Hocktide celebrations can be wit-
nessed at Hungerford, Berkshire ; one of the "Tuttimen" claims his kiss from a resident.*

OAK APPLE DAY IN DERBYSHIRE

The villagers of Castleton, in Derbyshire, celebrate Oak Apple Day, or Royal Oak Day, which commemorates the escape in 1651 of Charles II after the Battle of Worcester.

OAK APPLE DAY IN WILTSHIRE

Oak Apple Day, which falls on May 29, is also an occasion in the pretty village of Wishford, in Wiltshire. A group of revellers pass by the thirteenth century church.

SWAN-UPPING ON THE THAMES

The old practice of " upping " the swans on the River Thames has been carried on through the last four centuries. All the swans on the river between London Bridge and Henley are owned by the King and the Dyers' and Vintners', two of the oldest trade companies of the City of London. Once every year the official swan-markers go up the Thames in boats to take up the cygnets and mark their beaks to distinguish rightful ownership. The Royal Swan Warden attends the proceedings in a special barge, manned by a crew of three and flying two flags. Each of the Companies' boats, too, carries its own flag, that of the Vintners' bearing three tuns and the Dyers' three bundles of wood. The chief swan-markers wear traditional jerseys of red and white or blue and white stripes. The " upping " of hundreds of swans always lasts several days.

MAY DAY FESTIVITY

The First of May, especially in Elizabethan times, was widely observed as a public festival. In towns and villages processions were formed and dancing on the green around the maypole took place. After the Civil War the Roundhead Parliament, in 1644, forbade the erection of maypoles, but they returned to favour at the Restoration and in 1661, under the personal supervision of James II, who was then the Duke of York and Lord High Admiral, a maypole 134 feet in height was set up in the Strand. To-day, though of less significance than in years gone by, May Day festivities are still widely practised, especially in country districts. In the procession shown the maypole precedes the May Queen through the Bedfordshire village of Elstow, which was the birthplace of John Bunyan and is situated in the farming districts of the south midlands.

MAY DAY AT MINEHEAD

In the old town of Minehead, Somerset, May Day is celebrated with a curious hobby-horse (left) which parades through the streets to the accompaniment of tunes played on the concertina and drums. The weird costume of the Minehead hobby-horse is actually supposed to represent a ship with the tail of a cow attached to it. This is said to owe its origin to the sinking of a ship on the eve of May Day 1722, when the only object washed ashore was a dead cow. A hobby-horse is also used on May Day at Padstow, Cornwall.

MORRIS DANCERS

At Bampton, a village to the west of Oxford, there has been a troupe of Morris dancers for the past six hundred years. Each year on May Day they perform in Oxford City. Morris dancers are always distinguished by their white shirts and white flannel trousers. On their legs they wear pads which carry bells.

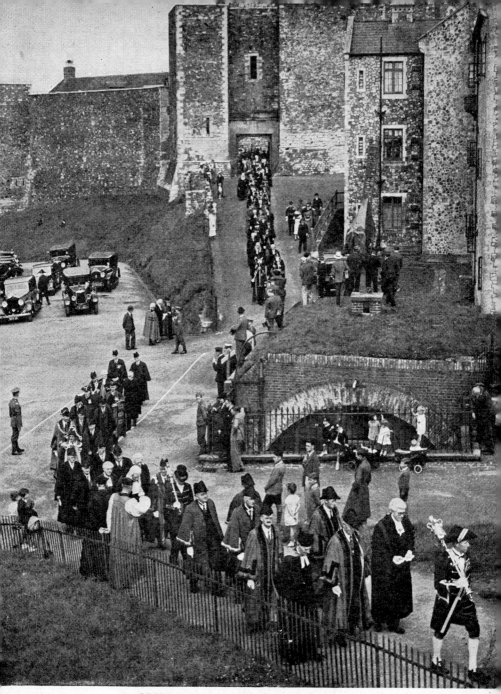

CEREMONY AT DOVER CASTLE

A new Lord Warden of the Cinque Ports is installed at Dover Castle. The Cinque Ports are towns along the south-east coast of England which, during the Middle Ages, enjoyed special privileges in return for supplying ships for the Navy. Dover, Sandwich, Romney, Hythe and Hastings were the original Ports to which Rye and Winchelsea were added.

TOWN CRIERS' CONTEST

Town criers still perform useful duties in many parts of England, as for centuries past, and once a year they gather at Pewsey, in Wiltshire, for a competition held to judge the clearest voice and best delivery. Here are some typical criers in performance.

TWO LONDON CUSTOMS

In the picture above officials at the Tower of London are seen tasting the Bragget, a secret brew of ale which has been made there for some three hundred years. Below, annual procession of the Vintners' Company headed by two wine porters sweeping before them.

ANCIENT COUNTRY CUSTOMS

A curious old custom takes place every Whit Monday on Cooper's Hill, Gloucestershire. A large round cheese is set rolling down the steep grassy slope and the local lads then chase after it. Whosoever manages to get the cheese first claims it together with a small money prize. There are six races, one of them reserved for the girls only. Here the master of ceremonies (in top hat and white smock) has just given the word " Go." Ancient custom gives Furry dancers the right to pass in and out of shops and houses on their way down the High Street of Helston, Cornwall, top right. Probably a survival of some pagan spring festival, the Furry dance has taken place annually for many centuries. The Tichborne Dole, bottom right, has been in existence for eight centuries and is distributed in the Hampshire village on March 25th every year. Sir Anthony Tichborne, the present Lord of the Manor, is seen helping to measure out the gifts of flour to his tenants on the steps of Tichborne House. Every man receives one gallon of flour while the women and children get half a gallon each. Before the flour is given away it is blessed by the Tichborne family chaplain during a short service held at the village church.

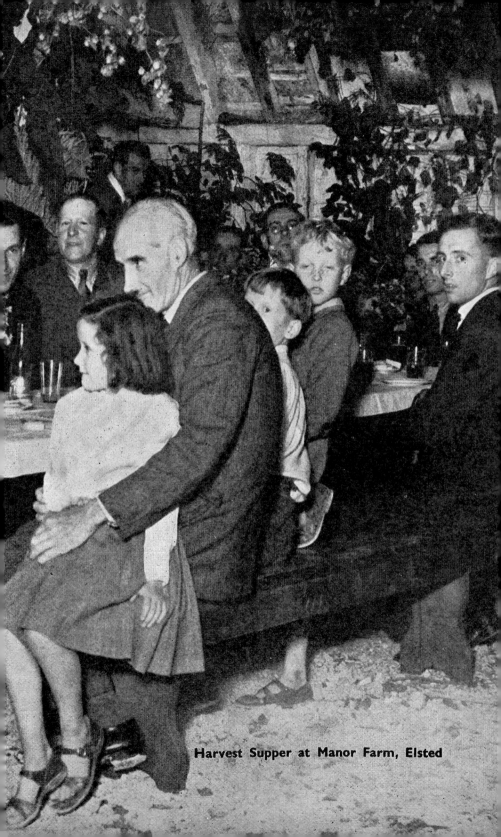

Harvest Supper at Manor Farm, Elsted

HARVEST CUSTOMS

Many interesting old customs are associated with harvest-time in England, chief of which is the Harvest Festival in the town and village churches. On the left a boy is seen handing a sheaf of corn to the vicar of Farnham, in Surrey, before the annual ceremony of Blessing the Crops. Below, a mammoth loaf of bread and a huge Cheddar cheese being carried in procession to the vicarage garden of East Brent, in Somerset, for the Harvest Home celebrations. The ceremony also includes a procession of the local housewives, each carrying a home-made pie or plum pudding to the vicar. All the gifts are later sold or distributed among the poorest parishioners.

HORN-DANCERS OF STAFFORDSHIRE

At Abbots Bromley, in Staffordshire, the Horn-Dancers make merry early in September. The ancient custom is a survival from the days when the Normans ruled England, and is supposed to commemorate the granting of hunting rights in the old Forest of Needwood.

THE CHRISTMAS MUMMERS

Among the oldest outdoor ceremonies of Christmas-time are the performances of the village mummers. There are many troupes in the southern and Midland counties ; here is one in the market square at Marshfield, in Gloucestershire. These mumming rites have been handed down for eight centuries. The players perform a comic play.

Young England

A MAIN concern with the young of any land must be their up-bringing, which implies their education. Here attention is focused on some of the main features of the English education system, in which schooling is compulsory for all. Schooling often begins, if the parents desire, when the child is no more than two years old and goes to a nursery school; here the child meets others and is given things to do which both amuse and to some extent instruct. The state-controlled primary and secondary schools are the backbone of the education system. State control is exercised through local authorities. After leaving the secondary school, education can be continued in a variety of technical and county colleges which offer part and full time training for industry, commerce and the arts. For the young man or woman intending to enter one of the professions for which the possession of a degree is considered necessary there are numerous universities. There are also schools of other types, too numerous fully to explain, of which indication will be found in these pages.

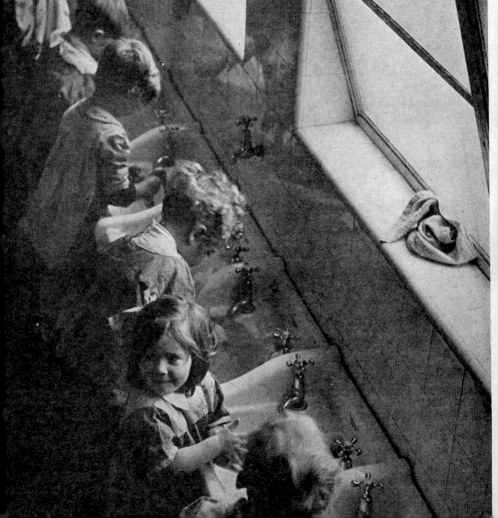

NURSERY SCHOOLS

There are now over one thousand nursery schools in England, the majority of which are provided by local education authorities. Attendance is not compulsory, but children are cared for by trained staffs in healthy and congenial surroundings. Children are introduced to a variety of play activities, both manipulative and creative, which both amuse and instruct. Training in good habits and right behaviour is given and there is free medical inspection, of which the results are communicated to the parents so that they may arrange treatment for any troubles discovered. Another important function of the nursery school is the provision of a good midday meal which is of great value to growing children. It is, of course, in the crowded cities, especially when the mother has to leave her child for long hours during the day, that the nursery school is of particular value.

FIRST LESSONS

From the age of five school attendance is compulsory for every child. Between the ages of five and eleven most children attend primary schools of which the majority, as also with secondary schools, are provided by local education authorities. Here young children listen eagerly to a story by their teacher in a modern primary school at Reading.

A PLAYGROUND IN THE PARK

Though some city streets are closed to traffic in order that they may be used as children's playgrounds, no one can regard such a device as satisfactory. Much better are the playgrounds now maintained by many municipal authorities in public parks and open spaces where children can play in safety. The playground shown is in St. James's Park, London.

CONTRASTS IN SCHOOLS FOR YOUNG CHILDREN

In the village school, such as that pictured on the facing page, accommodation is sometimes cramped ; one mistress may even have to conduct classes for children in two or three different age groups simultaneously in a single room. This is satisfactory neither for teacher nor pupils, but is occasioned by very real difficulty ; most village schools are old, the number of pupils small and there is a general shortage of teaching staff. By contrast the primary schools, such as that above, where pupils have lined up on the playground before filing into the classrooms, usually are of more recent construction and have been designed to accommodate large numbers of children ; facilities, accordingly, are in general, better.

SCHOOLDAYS ARE PLANNED

In thinly populated districts children may live where distance and lack of transport make the journey to school difficult. Where a child lives more than three miles from a school the local authority is required by law to provide transport. At left, children are seen entering a motor coach which will take them back to their homes after the day's work in school. Proper rest and exercise are necessary to children's health; below, children are resting after the midday meal and, at left, engaging in an impromptu game of cricket during the morning break.

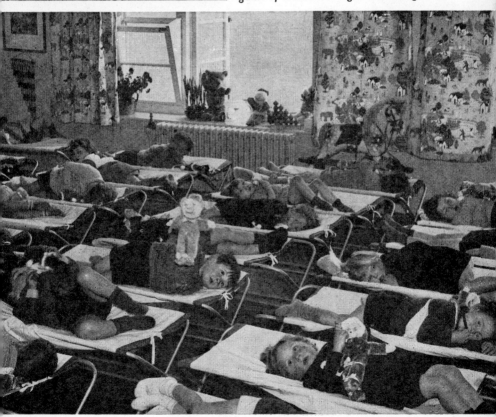

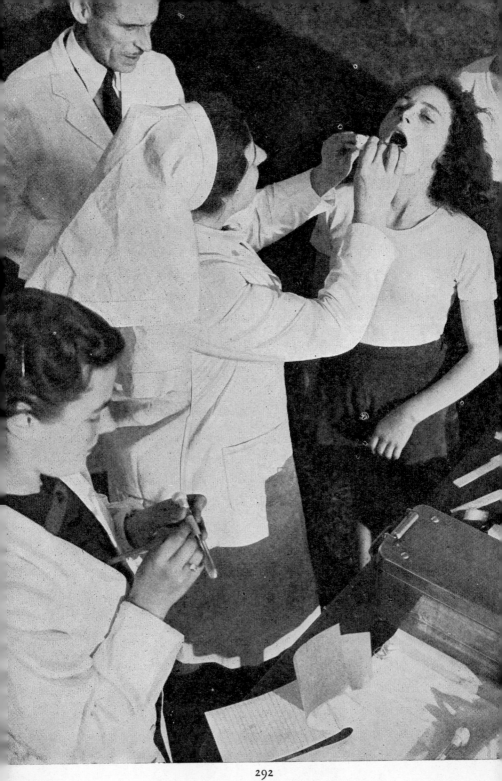

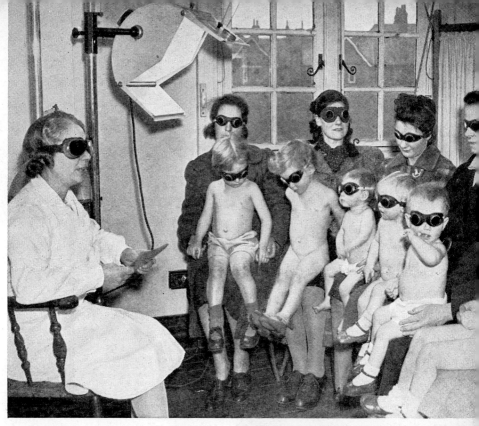

MEDICAL CARE IN SCHOOLS

All children attending State-provided schools undergo regular medical examinations, the results of which are reported to the parents, who can then obtain treatment through the local hospital. The great importance of this service is that it is instrumental in discovering trouble which, if undetected and so unchecked, would prove a source of handicap later in life. Considerable advance is being made also in the treatment of maladjusted children. Special schools are being provided both for children suffering from physical defects, which would handicap them in competition with normal children, and also, for mentally retarded children, who in a normal class would tend to hold back the development of others. Above is a health clinic where children are receiving sunray treatment, and, on the right, children are seen undergoing eyesight tests.

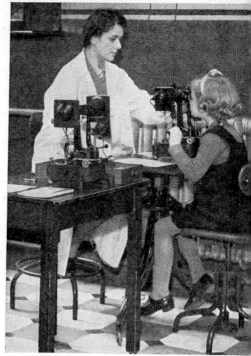

SCHOOLBOYS AT WORK AND PLAY

At the age of eleven or twelve pupils can pass from the primary to the secondary school. The term secondary includes three main types of school: the technical school which trains technicians and craftsmen for industry, the modern school, offering a general education with a wide range covering both literary and practical subjects, and the grammar school. Some of these last have been taken over and included among the State provided schools, others are independent of the local authority though most of them admit a proportion of scholars from primary schools even though the bulk of pupils are drawn from private preparatory schools. Above, pupils of a secondary modern school in the chemistry laboratory. Right, schoolboys off duty by Thames-side in London.

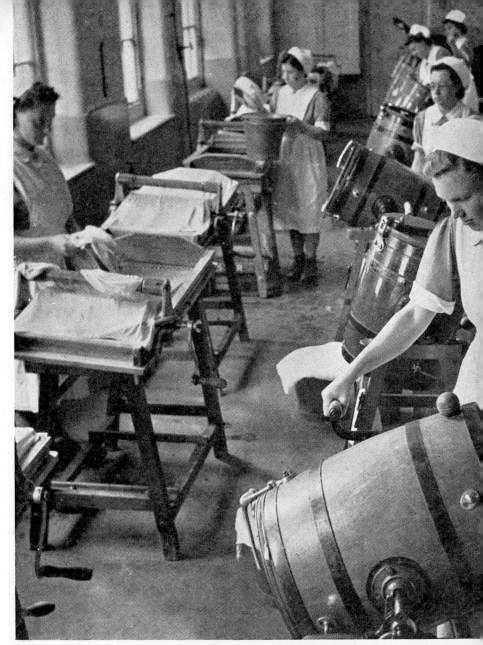

VOCATIONAL TRAINING FOR WOMEN

The great bulk of part-time vocational training offered in technical institutes and art colleges is still in the form of evening courses, but there has been a steady extending of the system whereby young employees are released by their firms during working hours for part-time attendance at technical colleges or other institutes. On these pages are shown classes in dressmaking, cooking and in the dairy. This last is part of a course in agriculture, lasting two years for a diploma, or three years for a degree, and leading to general employment either with the large dairy companies or the Government.

YOUTH AND THE ARTS

In many schools considerable attention is devoted to music and the fine arts and there is often a school dramatic society. The boys' orchestra of a secondary school in Ashford, Kent, is seen at practice at top left in the school music room. Below, young students at an evening art class criticize each other's work. Above, schoolboys Morris dancing.

England was the birthplace of the Boy Scout Movement. Since it was founded
in 1908 by Lord Baden-Powell, it has become the greatest international

WINDSOR CASTLE

youth movement. Above, led by Lord Cromer, the Chief Scout, nearly a thousand scouts cheer the King and Queen after a service at Windsor Castle.

ROLL CALL ON SPEECH DAY AT HARROW

Speech Day is one of the great occasions of school life. Often the scholars are privileged to hear an oration from an elder statesman or other notable figure from public life.

SPORT AT PUBLIC SCHOOLS

One of the features of life in public schools is the great attention which is paid to sport, especially to team games, such as cricket and football, which are regarded as a factor in forming the character. Above, a rugby football match is shown in progress at Oundle School, and below, a cricket match at Rugby School.

ENGLISH PUBLIC SCHOOLS

The English schools known as public schools are in fact private schools. They are fee-paying boarding schools independent of the local education authority and the headmaster of each is a member of the Headmasters' Conference. Many of these schools have proved themselves adaptable to the changing conditions of our time and scholarships are now available from secondary schools to a number of the public schools. On the left is the entrance to Blundells, an old-established public school for boys at Tiverton in Devon. Above, pupils in the library at Roedean School for girls, near Brighton.

ENGLISH UNIVERSITY LIFE

Dating from the thirteenth century, the Universities of Oxford and Cambridge are among the most respected centres of learning in the world. College life at a university affords more than learning alone ; valuable as are the facilities for specialized study, the rich cultural background resulting from participation in university life is an asset of definite, though incalculable, value in later life. On the left, undergraduates are about to dine in the Hall of King's College, Cambridge. Above, a corner of a study in Oxford University.

TRAINING FOR AGRICULTURE

On the farm the worker requires expert knowledge no less than the worker in the machine shop or factory and agricultural training is given in many schools as well as in special training centres. Above, boys on the Mammerton Farms in Derbyshire are changing the setting of the tool bar on a tractor. Mammerton Farms is one of four centres where boys receive preliminary training for farm work run by the Young Men's Christian Association. At left a schoolboy tends a young fruit tree. On the facing page student bee-keepers on the roof of the Goodall Road Senior Mixed School, Leyton : beekeeping is part of the school science curriculum.

BUILDERS IN THE MAKING

To assist in attracting boys to the building trades and in giving them proper training local educational authorities, in co-operation with the building industry, have set u schools which boys of thirteen can enter. Here, besides receiving instruction ordinary school subjects, pupils embark on a two-year course giving training various branches of building. At the end of the course, the boys can becom apprenticed to whichever building craft appeals to them. This scheme is in addition the practice whereby older boys can become apprenticed to master builders under t earn while you learn scheme of the building industry. On these pages pupils a shown receiving training in brick laying, above, and in architectural design, opposit

AT WORK ON A LATHE

Training in the use of machinery is now a regular part of instruction at technical schools; this student is using a lathe to cut metal tubing to precise dimensions.

TRAINING IN ENGINEERING

*An engineering student is finishing a pattern of a gear wheel. Later a cast will be made
in the metal shop ; for this to be satisfactory great accuracy is needed in the pattern.*

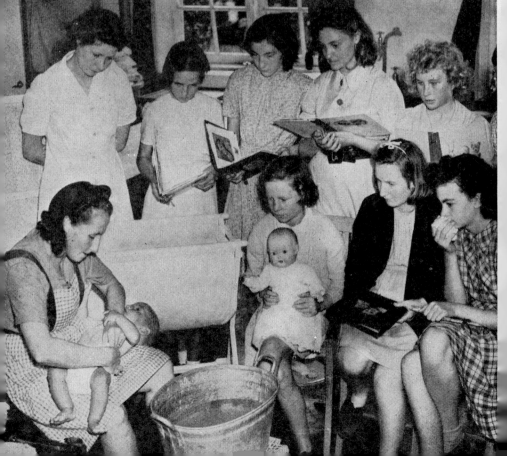

SPECIAL TRAINING FOR GIRLS

Nursing will always be one of the chief professions for women, and each of the large hospitals has its own training school where nurse probationers and nurses attend lectures. Lectures in mothercraft are given in many girls' schools. In the picture on the left a mother demonstrates the correct way to bath a baby, using her own as a model. Below, a girl training in the clock and watch industry is seen " true-ing " a clock spindle. Every prospective trainee in the clock factory undergoes an aptitude test, one part of which indicates the precision with which the hands can be used. On the right, this test is shown. A pencil point is suspended above a pattern on paper. By turning the handle the girl being tested moves the paper under the pencil point, and the accuracy with which she makes the pencil follow the pattern indicates her degree of precision.

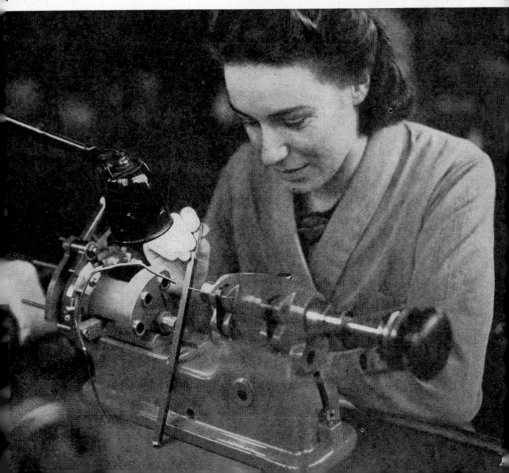

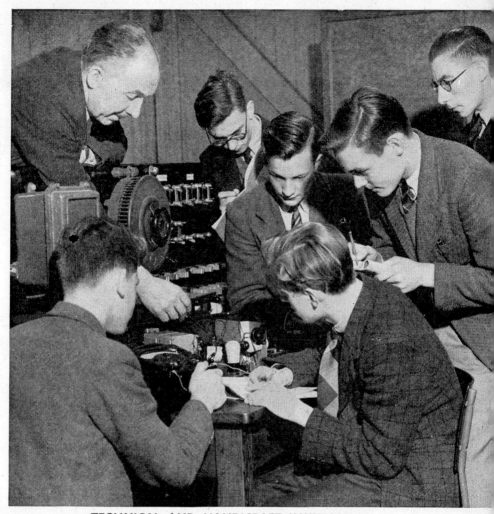

TECHNICAL AND HANDICRAFT INSTRUCTION

*Though not an integral part of normal education, both technical and handicraft instruc-
tion are available in a wide range of subjects. Technical students, like those above
learning to trace faults in wireless circuits on a course sponsored by the Ministry of
Labour at the South Essex Training College, usually have the definite objective of
employment in the field of their study, but the student of one of the handicrafts often
has a very different reason for learning. Handicraft training teaches the correct
way to use tools and encourages deft and precise use of the hands ; moreover, through
it lies a road to numerous hobbies of practical value and absorbing interest. On
the facing page, top, patterns in cut glass are being made at the Guildford School
of Arts and Crafts ; below, left, London County Council students of weaving at work
on a hand loom ; right, stitching the sections of a book before fitting the cover.*

POST SCHOOL

Education does not now necessarily stop when a child leaves school, especially as the need for trained personnel in industry and commerce is increasingly apparent. Courses usually are arranged rather by the concerns interested than by local education authorities. Students have for long been prepared for examinations such as those for banking and chartered accountancy, but the scope of post school vocational training

VOCATIONAL TRAINING

is extending. At top left, a class is in training for the Merchant Navy ; at bottom left, electrical engineering students are wiring the armature of an electric motor ; above, boys at a colliery training school in Yorkshire receive a first lesson in mine safety ; at top right, a class practises touch typewriting ; at bottom right, students in the Post Office training depot in Leeds study modern methods of handling mail.

END OF TERM

The year's work ends with parents attending the school speech day where awards for good work are presented and in the concert which often follows it is usual for the school choir to perform, as shown here at the North Ashford Central School for girls.

Published 1947.   T.347.T.   Printed by Keliher, Hudson & Kearns, Ltd., Hatfields, London, S.E.1.